Love in Action

Perspectives of the Prison System in America
from both sides of the walls

Order this book online at www.trafford.com
or email orders@trafford.com

Most Trafford titles are also available at major online book retailers.

Printed in the United States of America.

ISBN: 978-1-4269-2668-6 (sc)

Trafford rev. 02/06/2012

 www.trafford.com

North America & international
toll-free: 1 888 232 4444 (USA & Canada)
phone: 250 383 6864 ♦ fax: 812 355 4082

Foreword

Imagine the suffering of the myriads of people all over the world who have their loved-ones put away behind bars. Is it possible to keep a relationship that transcends all the barriers of prison walls, remote locations, the horrors of an inadequate prison system and that can sustain that connection over years and sometimes decades?

The answer is Yes. I discovered very soon the human potential of Dawud that I felt should not be wasted and the strength he would need to face his own past while weathering all the setbacks: the repeated denial of parole, the daily frustrations, the giving in to depression. I recognized Dawud from the start as my soul mate. The book makes clear the values I lived by, which gave me the strength to continue supporting him over three decades.

It wants to give courage to all those, who are languishing, either on this side or on the other side of the walls. We are all on a path of development. To believe in the higher self of the other as much as of one's own, isn't that another expression of LOVE? Real love can annihilate distances and make prison walls transparent. One can achieve ultimate wholeness together, even when cruelly separated from each other. That for me is the meaning of LOVE IN ACTION.

Contents

Chapter One

Setting the Tone

It was in 1979 in Jackson Prison, Michigan, that I saw Dawud for the first time. In the months and years that followed that first encounter, we both realized that we must have had met over many life times before. We immediately had such a rapport with each other that we could only marvel on the unbelievable feat of two people of such different backgrounds and circumstances being brought together: Dawud is in a prison in America, having grown up in a dysfunctional family; I was born and raised in the Netherlands in a warm family.

Preparatory Steps

Before I met Dawud I had already been five years in America, first in South Haven, Michigan, and from there in Kalamazoo and then radiating out in two directions, to work in Chicago and Detroit. In these two big cities I worked with inner city children, the ones who could easily end up in gangs and from there, in a downward spiral, become part of the prison system. I had a warm heart for those children. On the weekends, I would go to Kalamazoo, halfway in between those two cities, and restore my house, which was located in the black neighborhood "on the other side of the tracks". I had bought my house as a bargain opportunity with the idea of transforming it into a Eurythmy [1] Center. Living in a black neighborhood brought me some very different life experiences. I had to see with my own eyes how the black people, especially the males, were always watched by the police and, at the first (or without any) provocation, would be taken into custody.

I had grown up in the Netherlands in a family where the concept of racism was non-existent. I grew up with the notion that all people were equal and needed to be treated with respect. Here in America things were different, too obvious not to notice. Living in the black neighborhood in Kalamazoo as the only white person and, at that, a female, was a novelty for the black people but also put me on a steep learning curve. Some people may have called my attitude naive, and, from a certain aspect, it was, but it was based on a bigger image of the human being, with which I had grown up with.

First Encounter with Criminal Justice in America

In Kalamazoo I had gotten to know John, a black man from the South, whose street name was Alabama Slim, when my car had a flat tire near his gas station. While he went to fetch my tire, he left me with the open cash register and the task to pump gas for possible customers. I did not yet know that his job was a cover-up, arranged by the police to make him, a former drug dealer, inform on other drug pushers. He told me that he was thirty six and going to evening classes. I offered to help him with his English. Eventually, after some months, he ended up in prison, supposedly with a shorter sentence because of having been an informer. When I went to visit him in prison, I got my first inkling of how archaic the whole criminal justice system in America was. The reader may imagine how he, as an informant, was received by those he had snitched on and who had already served part of their sentences. His life was at risk, so he was put in an isolation cell. He was there six weeks, in which time I paid him my first visit. He was extremely nervous and scared to death to be brought into the visitor's room. You could scarcely have a conversation with him as he was like a hunted animal. He told me that he had not been given any underwear and the boots did not fit him at all.

Next thing, going through his records, the prison authorities discovered that he had had asthma as a child. They started treating him for asthma which he did not have any more. The result was that he got asthma so badly that they took him into the prison hospital. There he spent the next six weeks. After all these weeks in relative quiet, he was brought back into the general inmate population. Because of the overcrowding, they assigned him a bed in the new type of 'dormitories', where the bulkhead of each corridor was filled with bunk beds three high. Now he still had to face the anger of the former dope dealers. This experience gave me a first inkling of how inefficient and illogical the prison system is. The inmate is no more than a pawn in a game of chess. Any responsibility for his own life has been taken away from him!

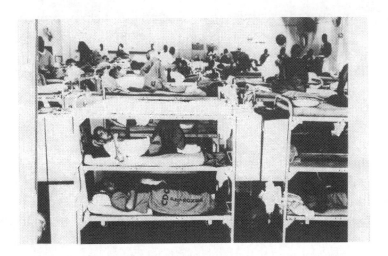

Doing Eurythmy in the Mackinac Prison

I visited John at first in jail, then in Jackson Prison. He had been transferred half a year later to the Mackinac Prison in the Upper Peninsula. It is a specialty of the prison system to build the prisons, where no other jobs are available. Building a prison creates the possibility for many people to work as guards. Never mind that the prisons are erected far away from the urban centers, where the prisoners originally came from, and that they hardly ever can have a visit from a family member. In the Mackinac Prison John started to tell some inmates about me and that I might be willing to do a workshop in Eurythmy, a kind of meditation in movement, with those inmates, who were inclined to try it out. John only knew that he respected me, so everything that came from me, even if he did not have much of an inkling about it, should be good.

Eurythmy requires at least four years of study. After that one may choose to go into the direction of becoming a stage performer, work as an educational Eurythmist in Waldorf or other schools, or choose to become a therapeutic Eurythmist. I embraced all of these directions, seeing in each of them the healing aspect. Eurythmy is like a universal language in movement whereby the expression of soul and spirit are as important as the bodily expression. It was a new thing for me to try to do this also in a prison setting. I knew it would have a healing quality for those who chose to be part of it, but it was a new undertaking.

Permission from the warden was received, and so my first session was announced for 8:00 am on a Monday morning! Going there meant a bus ride of fourteen hours, so I had to come a day early and stay in a motel for the night. Because of the fact that the prison was so far away, I could do this only once a month. I ended up with eight black male prisoners in a big gym, most of whom had "served" already years of their life sentences for crimes ranging from rape to murder. People often have asked me if I was not afraid to go into such a situation. It never entered my mind as I was full of trust and confidence that this was indeed a worthwhile thing to do. So I told the guard that it was OK for him to leave. In hindsight I know, it was a mistake to let the guard go, as he would have benefited from seeing these inmates, for once in a different light. Guards need as much soul food and inspiration as their wards. The prisoners appreciated the workshops very much. Their comments spoke to that. "This is something for real" they said. "If we only had done this when we grew up we would never have landed here". Their own education had been so dismal that they had never even heard the word POEM. The Eurythmy really resonated with them. After some very worthwhile sessions the prison authorities cancelled the work because I had had the audacity, in addition to doing the workshops, to visit individual inmates, who never got a visit from anyone.

Fighting the Reinstatement of the Death Penalty

Before even meeting Dawud I had started to take classes at Wayne State University in Detroit, relating to Criminal Justice issues. At the same time I discovered a group of lawyers, mostly Quakers, who put in a big effort against the reinstatement of the Death Penalty in Michigan. I found this an extremely worthwhile cause. As a Eurythmist, I was a little out of place amidst this group of lawyers, but they soon found the right job for me. They asked me to interview some twenty men and women who all had life sentences. If Michigan had had the death penalty and consequently death rows in their prisons, they would have been on Death Row or would already have been executed by the state.

It was my intention to show that so-called "murderers" are also people. I interviewed Tom, who had murdered his father who had been bullying him with physical force since he was a small boy. Finally when he was seventeen and strong enough to defend himself, he could not take the abuse any longer and fought back. As a result his father died. When I met him, he had already spent twenty-two years in prison. He told me: "I guess that you have already noticed that I have not become institutionalized at all, though I have been here far beyond the time limit where others have been turned into departmental robots. This is because I have the unique ability to retreat into my inner self. I also have a probing mind and know: Whatever changes occur within the Criminal Justice Department, they are not processed to rehabilitate, nor is it done with the interest in mind of protecting society from further crime. Quite the contrary! The Administrative Master Plan is for inmates to return to prison, once they are officially released. This process is induced by means so subtle, as only an alert mind can discover. The mind is the only weapon that you have to defend yourself, while you are in one of these human warehouses." If Michigan had had the death penalty, he would have been on death row.

When I tried to collect signatures from my fellow students in the Criminal Justice class at the university against capital punishment, all were *in favor of* the Death penalty. I felt that we had an uphill battle to fight. Yet we won, and the death penalty was not reinstated. At least not for the next four years. We humans are very concerned when animal or plant species are on the brink of becoming extinct. As man is a species onto himself, we should be equally concerned when we kill a person because he has killed, without trying to understand the deeper motivations to his deeds and his character. "Love in Action" is the attempt to understand the depths of one man, Dawud's being, the real person who came with a life's task but got so waylaid that his real being was overwhelmed, and he resorted for many years to use the lower road. Most important, this book hopes to show that transformation is possible, even in career criminals.

The Chance Meeting with Dawud

The Eurythmy workshops with prisoners was a consequence of my meeting and subsequent visits with Alabama Slim. When I was unable to continue with that,

I still wanted to be involved with this kind of work. I had inherited a small amount of money after my mother's death and put that to use by starting to work as a volunteer with an Ex-Offender Agency in Detroit. Many of the activities had to do with counseling inmates in prison or upon their release. The counseling sessions I was to conduct were mainly in Jackson Prison, a complex that houses some 5,000 inmates. The prison had just survived a huge riot. As soon as the situation had calmed down and was somewhat normalized, I was able to see inmates on an individual basis. Near the main entrance was a winding staircase that led to the mezzanine. Here only ministers and representatives of agencies could see inmates. I would have a list of names and numbers of inmates, who, one by one, would be called up.

After I had seen several inmates who were all on my list, an inmate walked up the staircase and towards me. I ask him, "Are you on my list of people to see?"

"No," he says, "I am out of bounds. I prayed since several days that I might come into contact with someone who would be very important for me." I asked why he came up the stairway then. "I was guided to go this way even though I am not supposed to be here at all. If they find out, I'll be in the hole on bread and water."

"What are you doing here then?" I asked. His answer: "I want to serve God". Then he asked me why I was there. "Most likely for the same reason", I said, "to serve God." He quickly handed me a slip of paper with his name and prison number on it with the request to visit with him in the visiting room.

After all the proper arrangements had been made, which took a couple of weeks, I finally sat face to face with him in the visitor's room. I was immediately baffled by his intelligence. I was able to discuss things with him I had not been able to discuss with anyone in America before. No one I spoke to had ever heard of Viktor Frankl*. It turned out that Frankl was our common hero. This made a big impression on me. I had finally found a person, of all places in prison, who had read all the books of Viktor Frankl.

Special Visitor

A good friend of mine, Erwin, came for a few weeks from Holland to America to give workshops at the Waldorf Institute in Detroit, where I also was teaching. As a young man he had had the deep wish to work with juvenile delinquents. But life's circumstances lead him in another direction. When he heard about my connection with Dawud, he immediately expressed the wish to visit him in Jackson prison. First, arrangements had to be made to get his name approved on Dawud's visitors list, but, after that, we were able to go. From the start of the visit Erwin was not, in any kind of way, intimidated by the whole way the guards handled the come and go of visitors and inmates. Neither was he disturbed by the intense noise level in the visiting room. I somehow contribute this high noise level to the feeling of discomfort people have with each other in such a setting. The prisoners are happy about getting a visit, but they hate the circumstances under which this has to take place. The family is agonizing about the fact that this person has been taken away from them. All of them, family and prisoners, have had already a long waiting period before they were finally brought together in the visiting room. The children were allowed to visit their fathers, but one could see how deeply affected they were to see them in this totally dependent situation.

When we were finally assigned our seating in the visiting room and Dawud came in, we could see the deep joy in Dawud's eyes, not only to see me but to get to know this, as of yet, unknown person. They hit it off very well. Very soon they were engaged in an intensive discussion about the Christ. Dawud was already enamored at that time with the Muslim religion. Knowing that, this kind of talk was all the more remarkable. After they had talked for a while, Erwin suggested that Dawud and I should have some time by ourselves without him. He wanted to go and sit somewhere else. I immediately told him that this was not allowed under any circumstance. His reply: "Never mind, I can do this." As he got up to sit somewhere else, I looked anxiously in the direction of the guar to see, how he would react. Against all the rules of the game, the guard did nothing and left him alone. Later on Erwin joined us again and after a while the time for the visit was up. We said good-bye to Dawud. He went back into the belly of the beast and we went outside. Nine years later Dawud wrote about the visit with Erwin:

"Even though Erwin met Dawud only once, I sensed a very special connection between them. That's why I read with keen interest what he had to say about people 'who consciously take on a dark karma in order that they gain the moral strength in themselves to overcome the darkness'. First of all, I don't (necessarily) think that anyone who has a sound mental and emotional constitution is going to consciously choose to live such a tormented and heartrending life as mine. That doesn't make a whole lot of rational sense. However, on the other hand, since one's true spiritual identity dwells in the subconscious, I can really endorse this statement, because for the last couples of years my life has become a living testament of this endeavor. I say this with the absolute assurance of now knowing what true morality is. For me it began on the day that I consciously made the decision to not ever (intentionally) hurt anyone again."

For Erwin the visit at the prison was not over yet. He wanted to take in the enormity of this place, in the realization that this prison warehoused 5000 inmates. So he expressed to me the wish to walk around the prison walls to take a closer look. Next to the entrance was one of the guard towers. On the grass was a sign saying: 'It is forbidden to walk beyond the paved walk way. Guards will shoot at any trespassers.' With the same inner certainty with which Erwin had reacted in the visitors room, when I told him he had to stay on his assigned seat, he now said: "Oh no, it's OK, I can do that." And he did and I with him. We did not walk all around the prison but far enough to get a good impression of this most forbidden place and what it could possibly mean to be put away for years and years, often for a life time, in little cubicles in this concrete bunker. As much as the prison made a deep impression on Erwin, he made a deeper impression on me.

Over a period of thirty years Erwin has continued to be interested in Dawud, to ask about his well-being, and has accompanied him in thought on the long process of his transformation. Even when Erwin's health was failing, and he got weaker by the day, his mind was as clear as a bell. In his last phone call before his death a week later, he expressed his support for this book, as he hoped it would help to bring out the true reality of this person, by the name of Dawud. And that it will also be a contribution for those people, who have so little belief in themselves and their ability to change, that they can not imagine anyone with that kind of a record could possibly change.

Handbook for Prisoners

I continued to visit Dawud a few times a month. Meanwhile, in my position of working with the Ex-Offender Agency, I had started to write regular articles in a kind of "Handbook" which was distributed once a month in several prisons in Michigan. The articles brought many positive responses from the inmates. Topics would be: "How to be Honest with Yourself*", "Viktor Frankl"*, "Human Dignity", "Is there Any Hope?", "On Guns", or "Who is Man?" The inmates found the Handbook a blessing. I just came across an article that Dawud wrote, basically summing up in 33 points* the drudgery and debasement of prison life. The article I wrote about Viktor Frankl had special meaning for Dawud and me. Many readers may be aware of the fact that Viktor Frankl spent many years in Auschwitz. His crime? Belonging to the Jewish race. Frankl, a psychiatrist, was able to extract from his terrible suffering a whole new philosophy which became known as Logotherapy*.

"There is nothing conceivable that would so condition a man as to leave him without any freedom", was one of his poignant statements. Dawud so admired Viktor Frankl that it gave him strength to cope with the debasement of prison life from day to day, from hour to hour.

The two books which made Viktor Frankl famous were Man's Search for Meaning and The Will to Meaning*. I used to compare the basic tenet of these two books with Rudolf Steiner's "Philosophy of Freedom" *. Frankl and

Steiner knew that insight alone was not yet enough to give meaning to life. The will has to be engaged to act upon the insight.

Multi-Talented Friend

How was Dawud able to discuss these books in depth with me? It turned out that he had read most of the classics while he was still in the Ionia Reformatory in Northern Michigan. To his great advantage a wealthy businessman had—upon his death—left his whole personal library to that prison. Dawud, who as a boy had had such an aversion to school that he mostly played truant, found a new urge to read. For weeks and months he would bury himself in the books and absorb them all. In the beginning it might take him a couple of hours to struggle through one page, but—as he kept at it—he was able to give himself a belated education. Dawud also baffled me, for instance, with his deep familiarity with Shakespeare.

Not only could I discuss any topic with him, he also showed me photos of paintings he had made in prison and subsequently sold to guards or instructors. They were highly original and well executed. Another unusual thing was that for years Dawud had played classical guitar, whereby the majority of inmates were only interested in rock and roll or heavy metal. The reader may wonder how Dawud got a classical guitar, as he never got anything from his family. He was able to earn money with his art work but also had a way to convince the guards to do him special favors.

When I met Dawud in 1979, he had already spent ten years in Jackson Prison. Most of the inmates did not have much of any work assignments. That's how Dawud could devote so much time to this art work and to his music. Dawud had something refined about him. Already, as a small child he would turn on the radio to listen to classical music. He was repeatedly and rudely pulled away from this activity by his mother, because "boys don't listen to that stuff."

Dawud did other unusual things. He was the only one amidst 5000 inmates who had the idea of having a garden and growing vegetables. Somehow, he was able to convince a few guards to bring him seeds. From somewhere he organized to get a spade or a rake, and every day during air time he would be busy in his garden. I know of other places like the jail in Oakland where growing vegetables has been used as a healing tool for inmates to develop a love for nature as well as earning them a little money. Dawud created this healing tool for himself and had a way to get into constructive conversations with some other prisoners who at first had looked with disdain at such an undertaking as being sissy-stuff.

I met in him, in this most unlikely setting an intelligent, creative person, well-versed both in the visual arts and in music. I saw so much talent. He also had perfected his writing skills over the years. Even the professor who graded his paper while he took college classes in another prison, commented on this. "If only my graduate students would write papers like this, I would be very happy."

So far I had only experienced his world as he presented himself inside the visiting room and through his letters. Bit by bit I would start to understand what energy Dawud needed to create such capacities in the face of day-to-day prison life. Here are, as a sample, three points of the "33 Ways to Play a Loser's Game" *written by Dawud for the Handbook.

1. There will be absolutely no privacy, and you can expect to do "hard time" in a hostile environment.

2. Don't expect the twisted circumstances of imprisonment in themselves to improve anyone's character or disposition. Since association is forced and limited by the very nature of the prison situation some of your companions will oscillate between explosive bad temper and boisterous annoyance. Others will unapproachably withdraw to the point of being totally uncommunicative.

3. In Prison we have been thrust into an abnormal twilight zone where neurosis, psychosis and paranoia reign supreme. You are to be pitied if you expect any meaningful interest in you or your problems.

At the same time Dawud could write "Unicorns Are Real", which shows a very sensitive soul, who was forced to conjure up other worlds than what he experienced from day to day in the prison life around him.

Unicorns Are Real

Do you remember when nothing seemed impossible? When you could reach out and touch forever? I wish to return to that time when I could see sound, listen to colors, feel the thoughts of trees, and be at the beginning and end of time simultaneously and know these things were possible.

No one had ever told me that I could not become flowing water or the shadow of the wind if I wished.

No one had told me that I could not fly with the falcons, or do eurythmy in a dungeon.

No one had told me that fire flies were not stars that had tired of standing in one place and had come down to dance with me.

No one told me that I could not run naked with the wolves, or that I could not walk on a rainbow to the sun's side of the clouds and return to the earth in my lover's tears.

No one had told me! So I did these things without questions. I was part of everything in the world and everything was part of me.

I wish to be that sure of life again, to see behind the past and beyond the future; to know that Unicorns are real and we'll be together in the after world.

After all the reader has heard of my stories about work with 'black' children, youth and adults, they probably assume that Dawud was black too. Of all the people I met on the mezzanine that fateful day in 1979, Dawud was the only 'white' person.

Born on the Same Day!

I felt that we had so much in common. Each meeting was like a meeting of soul mates. I actually was convinced that we had been twins in a former life. How baffled I was to find out that Dawud's birthday was exactly on the same day as mine! How could that possibly be true? Was there a deeper meaning to this? We had the same birthday, the "only" difference being that he was eighteen years younger than I. In each subsequent visit as well as in his letters, Dawud started talking about the parole date that was due and his possible release. He wanted to get married with me as soon as he would be free. I hesitated for a long time but finally decided that it would be to Dawud's advantage to live like a "proper citizen". We had discussed already many details—it was supposed to be a Muslim wedding!—and had set the date for it. I am a Christian and member of the Anthroposophical Society, and was not especially interested in a Muslim wedding. But the Muslim faith meant a lot to him. As a prison counselor I had met many Muslims who had quite a good outlook on life. They were given specific directions how to conduct themselves, and, most of all, they were given a lot of support while in prison and upon their release. So I went along with the idea of a Muslim wedding. However, when the date for Dawud's possible parole came around, he was given an extension of his sentence.

This is quite a normal procedure for prisoners to be reviewed for parole year after year, but I did not know that. Prisoners always have their hopes up, mostly to be dashed again and again. The date for the wedding was set. The big change now was that the wedding was to take place in the prison!

Truus Geraets

24

Dawud had made the arrangements for an Imam to perform the necessary duties. I invited some Muslim friends, who were studying to become Waldorf teachers. Dawud invited some friends from within the prison. We included as part of the invitations a Russian Legend*: "Who are the Chosen Ones?"*(See Appendix)

The content in short is: "To whom then are open the gates of paradise?" The answer is basically that the gates of paradise are open to all who are suffering and thus have exhausted themselves, or who have compassion for those who are suffering, a heart that offended, almost consuming itself for grief, a heart that is willing to take on even the greatest sin for the sake of the divine light, a heart that is trying to do God's will. The story is actually much longer. It reminds me of words by Goethe*, who said:

"The new religion must be fashioned from ugliness, death, sin, crime and poverty. It is they who teach us to love the Divine."

I bought Dawud a wedding outfit and sent it to him by mail well in advance. On the day itself, all the guests had to be frisked and fingerprinted and leave their belongings at the front desk. When I finally saw Dawud, he was not wearing the special outfit I had sent him. His only comment: "O yes, someone has stolen it already." For him, it was not a big deal:, for me it was another of the initial little shocks.

Chapter Two

The Beginning of Waiting for Dawud

"If you want to lift a person out of the scum and dirt, don't just stretch out your hand and try to pull him up. You have to go down into the mud and scum yourself and then raise him and yourself together to the light."

From Hassidic Sayings (Rabbi Solomon)

Here I was, married but not really married, as I was still living all by myself. The set-off was at least for a year with no guarantee that Dawud would be paroled then. I decided to try and get an appointment with the Chairman of the Parole Board in Michigan. One week before Christmas 1980 I had my audience with him. On his desk before him were big files containing Dawud's criminal records. Dawud had told me some things of his past but not even a tenth of what I was going to hear then from the mouth of the Chairman of the Parole Board. I can't remember the details, but it was quite shocking. I still asked the Chairman if he had ever met Dawud in person. He denied that. I, obviously, went into the celebration of Christmas with a heavy heart. After some two weeks, I had collected my wits enough to write a very short letter to the Chairman, basically saying that all the knowledge he had was only obtained from dusty old records.

I challenged him to go and see Dawud and meet him in person.

This is not the usual procedure, as the reader may imagine, that a family member—in this case the wife of a prisoner—challenges the all powerful Chairman of the Parole Board to review his final decisions. The Chairman went, indeed, in person to see Dawud and had a congenial conversation with him. As a result of that, he released him much earlier. This is so unusual and unique that the Chairman would change his mind, even after a final decision had been made to keep someone locked up. In later years and in other settings, when Dawud had again and again been denied parole, I was many times tempted to perform the same feat again, but knew this was so unique and could only be done successfully once.

Young People at Risk

What I have discussed so far may show that I had every intention to work with young people at risk, with people who found themselves on the other side of the law. I had developed quite a reputation as such. From out of my therapeutic background and my work in special education, I brought to this interest the wish to help young people to overcome their anger, their disgruntledness with society. Already in the Esperanza School in Chicago, a Waldorf Day School for handicapped children where I worked, we had many youngsters whose brothers and sisters were in the gangs. They were a daily challenge. I learned from them as they learned from me. So when I was invited to Houston, Texas, to do some work with a group of some thirty juvenile delinquents between the ages of fourteen and twenty, I responded to the challenge. They all had committed crimes, serious enough to have been taken into custody. As I entered the room where I was to meet them, I saw how they were all slumped on lounge chairs with expressions of total disinterest. The only way I could reach them was to let them feel that I somehow understood them. When the gentleman, who had organized this session, also tried to join in talking to them, I had, in the most polite way, to tell him to shut up, as his words put the youngsters off and made them withdraw even further into their own worlds. It was a situation for me of swimming or drowning. I could not risk loosing them. After the initial talk and a few words about the merit of Eurythmy, I invited them to get up and join me for some exercises. I was lucky enough to get about one third of them to respond. After about five minutes of doing this I asked them to tell a bit about the realities of their lives. Through the movement exercises some of the initial reluctance to get involved had loosened up. It was clear that doing these movements had touched some deeply hidden positive source that had slumbered within, waiting to be released. After that more of the young people were willing to join in the next round of exercises. This is an amazing phenomenon, the redemption of the spirit, which can be freed in a person who is willing to move.

Young people experience deeply their loneliness and seek for community in the presence of their peers. The family structure has often broken down to such a degree that they are searching for a substitute family in the streets. Unless young people are given a direction by which they can orient themselves and can develop their own individuality, they will fall prey to the pressure asserted on them by their peers or by the media. It is there where the ground is prepared for criminal behavior. In doing Eurythmy they may have experienced, for a short moment, a real community spirit. It, obviously, needs a much longer exposure to activities that can lift them up in a way that is acceptable to them.

Dawud's Early Life Experiences

Martin Luther King said: "I have the audacity to believe that people everywhere can have three meals a day for their bodies, education and culture for their minds and dignity, equality and freedom for their spirits".

What happens to people when they are deprived of maternal love and guidance? Dawud's own mother had lost her mother very early. The father, at a loss what he should do with a little child while he drove trucks all over the US, had given his daughter into the care of nuns. When she was only fourteen, she ran away and got lost in a world she was incapable of handling. That made it also impossible for her to become a real mother for Dawud. Her second child, also a boy, was taken away from her by the social service and happened to be adopted by a sister of Dawud's father in Kentucky. Dawud's father, who basically was a good man, was incapable of bringing any order in this chaotic household and left his wife after a third child was born, a girl this time. Dawud may have been a child that nowadays would be called hyperactive. Both his mother and his step father were mostly drunk. His mother tried many times to get rid of her son by pushing the pram, for instance, with Dawud in it down the stairs. On a photo of Dawud as a six year old one sees him sitting on a swing with his left arm in a cast and looking totally dejected and without any interest in the world. He remembers this incident very well when his mother threw him down so hard that he broke his arm. At other times she punished him by holding his little hands above the flames of a gas burner. Still now Dawud can conjure up the smell of burning flesh. Whenever his mother had to take him to the hospital for again another injury, she would dream up some explanation of how he fell out of the tree or had played with fire.

I need to warn the reader as to what is following. Writing about Dawud's youth does not allow for pretty tales. In addition to what his mother did to him was the treatment he got from his uncle. When his mother and step father were working, Dawud was left in the care of this uncle. Dawud had to undergo the worst sexual abuse which always came with threats of: "If you ever dare to tell anyone . . ." And then there was his grandfather who was finally going to teach this unruly boy some lessons he would never forget. He somehow knew that Dawud was afraid of the dark. He already had threatened him again and again by saying that he would call the Boogeyman who would then take care of him. One afternoon the uncle took the boy by the arm and dragged him into a dark closet and locked the door. The more Dawud cried and screamed, the more intensive he would make the frightening noises a Boogeyman is supposed to make. Dawud, still being a child with a lively imagination, could only believe that the Boogeyman was indeed coming to get him. The grandpa would go away for a while but always came back with these blood curling screams a Boogeyman is supposed to make. This went on for the whole night. Finally when Dawud was released from his dungeon, he had lost his speech. For three years he never spoke a word. What did they not do to this child to put him on the way towards becoming a professional criminal?

<u>In His Own Words*</u>

"I was raised in the all American dysfunctional family. Both my mother and stepfather were alcoholics and emotionally retarded. As role models they did not possess a single redeeming quality that I wanted to emulate. To this day, I can't recall a single conversation I had with either one of them in which they even made a half-hearted attempt to enlighten my conscience or steer me in a positive direction. Just to say that they allowed me to do whatever I damn well pleased to do, would be an understatement. When I was eleven, because of excessive truancies, multiple thief charges and repeated run-aways from home, the Juvenile Court intervened and switched primary custody to my real father. In 1960 I went to live with them and his new family, consisting of my stepmother, who was in her late twenties, my stepbrother, who was five and stepsister who was three. This was in Kentucky. I fell in love with my stepmother overnight, as she was charming, smart as a whip and had a delightful sense of humor. She became my first real friend and was ten times the mother to me than my real mother ever was. My father worked the evening shift, so throughout the week I would only see him during supper. Although he was a man of few words and a firm disciplinarian, he had a gentle loving spirit and to this day I cannot say one bad thing about him. I lived with them for three and half years, and it was the closest I have ever experienced to having a normal childhood."

Yet, also his father and stepmother had to give up on this unruly boy, no matter how they tried to help him. The damage to his psyche from the earlier years had taken its toll. So, when he was fourteen, his father took him back to live with his mother in Detroit. He spent the next two years in and out of Juvenile Hall, running the streets and gangbanging. Because Dawud was clearly a leader figure, he soon got into the position of becoming the leader of the gang, which went under the name of the "Stilettos".

First Prison Sentence

"The charge that took me to prison the first time was Armed Robbery, for which I received five years. Back in the mid-sixties, Ionia Reformatory in Northern Michigan was a brutal and eerie place. Even though I was the youngest inmate there, I quickly blended right in with the other misfits and hooligans. I got into a fight every day for the first three days and got my ass severely whipped, but I had passed muster, proving that I had heart; therefore, I was accepted into the fraternal order of the Brotherhood of the Damned. I was paroled nineteen months later. In retrospect of my first sentence, what stands out in my memory more than anything else, was that, when I got released in '67, I was much more criminally minded and twice as violent and aggressive than I had been when I went in. During the next three years I spent nearly all of it in prison, violating my parole twice."

Dawud finally landed in the State Prison of Southern Michigan, known as Jackson Prison.

How did he manage to not only survive his ordeal but also to find a light to open his mind in all these dreary years? This is how Dawud describes the Jackson prison experience himself:

"I was twenty-one when I arrived in Jackson Prison. Little did I know that I was entering a world where all my nightmares would come true, and I would witness and/or experience (like Dr. Frankl) man's cruelty in the extreme. During the mid-seventies, Jackson Prison had the highest murder rate of any prison in America. That's because it was wide open. Gambling was legal and drugs of every variety were plentiful. I have often been asked to describe what it was like to have lived in an environment where I witnessed almost as a daily occurrence: Men brutally stabbed and bludgeoned to death, thrown from the fourth tier (floor) of a cell block, burned to a cinder in a locked cell and savagely gang raped. I tell them that if they can imagine being on the front line during a fire fight, then that would be a fair similarity. In retrospect, the only explanation that I can give for having survived those extremely wild and violent years unscathed (at least physically) was that I must have a very powerful angel protecting me; considering that I was just as involved—more or less—in the prison' subculture, which caused me to have several life and death confrontations with my peers. After enduring eight years of this horror, I was transferred to a Trustee Camp, from where I escaped shortly thereafter. Two and a half days later I was apprehended with a pistol. Consequently I had five years added to my sentence."

Chapter Three

<u>Released at Last</u>

When I met Dawud in 1979 he had already spent some thirteen years in different prisons, nine of them in the State Prison of Southern Michigan, for short Jackson Prison. He was released in 1980—at the recommendation of the Chairman of the Parole Board! When I picked Dawud up from the prison, I took him straightaway into a nature experience. My thinking was that he had been locked up for so long in concrete bunkers, that this was the best way for him to connect directly to nature and use this as a start to make a new beginning in the free world. Part of Dawud's prison experience had been that he had spent fourteen months in solitary confinement. Each month the warden would come to suggest that he join again the general prison population, but Dawud was too defiant to give in. Being in an isolation cell means that one only has a slab of concrete to sleep on, that a light bulb is on 24 hours day and night and that there is one watering hole in the center, to be used as a toilet that flushes every 15 minutes or, if one is thirsty enough, to drink from. No books, not even a bible, no paper and pencil were deemed appropriate. Dawud discovered very soon that in order to survive this ordeal he had to become his own best friend. Some people get stir crazy after three days. When I heard that, I realized that Dawud was not going to be an ordinary person and that he probably would go his own way very strongly. This attitude was his strength but also would get him, over the years, in a lot of trouble and into ongoing long periods of renewed incarceration.

He was elated by the idea of going camping for a few days in Northern Michigan. In his long years in prison, in later years, he would always transport his mind back to this camping experience and mull over it, again and again. It made a deep impression on his psyche. Of the many adventures we had, one was to swim across the lake while transporting all our belongings, securely packed into plastic bags, on an air mattress. The idea was to set up camp on the other side of the lake. It was wilderness at its best. By now the reader may understand that Dawud had this wild streak and was very adventurous. Another day we rented a canoe in which we went down a fast current of a stream. We constantly had to dodge big trees which had fallen across the river. On other days Dawud used some of his surplus energy by going jogging long distance. I had not met any other people yet in this part of Saginaw County, but Dawud would find them and convince them that he urgently needed a joint to smoke. I only found out by finding the stub of the cigarette in his breast pocket. Later on, I did not need any evidence any more. I knew immediately when Dawud had smoked a reefer because he would talk fervently about all the plans he had. I recognized then slowly what they really were: pipe dreams, as he did not have the will then to follow up on them. That all would change in later years, but then

Dawud was still like a wild colt. He already had years of exposure to marijuana behind him which would extend to some 20 years. Later, but not in the time he was with me, he got hooked for three years on cocaine.

On hindsight, I can see that I had a very ideal picture of this multi-talented friend. I myself never touched alcohol, smoked ordinary or other cigarettes. I had written a whole article for the Prisoners Handbook about marijuana and what it does to your brain. My article was a warning to take this drug seriously, as it has the effect of shrinking your brain, but Dawud would not have it. According to him, it was nothing and why did I get worked up about this? After the wilderness adventure we tried to settle in my apartment in Detroit near Jefferson Avenue and the Detroit River.

Going Back to His Old Turf

I had to experience again and again that a person while he is locked up—incarcerated as it is called officially—is quite a different person from the one who, all of a sudden, is released and has to make it in the free world. I saw this with the many other ex-offenders, whoM I counseled. This, definitely, is a topic to be visited later on and to give in-depth attention to. For now on, I had Dawud to be concerned about.

I had no idea that he would first have to revisit and relive all his years on the streets of Detroit from the time before he got to prison. According to the parole plan he had to try and find work every day, but at that time Michigan had a very high unemployment rate. It was practically impossible for someone with a prison record to find work. They would hire him at first sight, as he can present himself well, but as soon as they checked up on him via his social security number, he would not get the job. Never dismayed about anything, Dawud created his own adventures. A few times he would not come home at night. I had no idea where he was. He tried to earn some money but not necessarily the usual way. In prison he had become very good at playing pool. People play for money. Normally you have that money in your pocket before starting to bet with it. Dawud would bet with no money to back it up in case he would loose. Sometimes he won, but when he lost he had to disappear from the scene, as the other players were going after him. He practically never came to rest and always was hyper nervous.

Detroit was known for being a city with high crime incidents. We lived not too far from the Detroit Waldorf School in the Indian Village where I taught Eurythmy. One night burglars stole all the violins and cellos of the children. When the people who were going to burglar proof the whole building had their cars parked outside, they were stolen too. From that time onward the school always had to have guards, watching the place and the safety of the children day and night.

Dawud had warned me that I should always give in when someone would accost me and demand that I give him my money. Typically for Dawud, when it happened to him, when he had $400 in his pocket, he did not follow up on his advice to me. When three black guys jumped him from behind the bushes he must have looked them straight in the eye. He heard them mumble: "He surely is a cop". They disappeared without any further to do. Dawud, obviously, had a lot of practice in staring people down and making sure that they better not mess with him. Each time that these and other things happened I kept the pure image of his being in a warm place in my heart.

Because Dawud had heard so much from me about Waldorf education, he went along with the idea to enroll in the Waldorf Teacher Training in Greenfield, Detroit. He lasted there only six weeks. He was somehow too nervous to sit quietly through lessons and take in much of its contents. He always had to run out to have a smoke. When it came to choosing a group of students with whom to bring the life and historic period of Harun al Raschid*, he was very enthusiastic to be involved with them. He had learned a lot of Arabic in prison and could imitate the muezzin calling the faithful to prayers. With all his creativity he was a welcome participant of that group. Much had still to happen over the years to calm him down. I was at the same time teaching Eurythmy at the Teacher Training. Dawud brought some embarrassment to me by getting too close to some of the female students.

Another more serious incident happened when one evening he was going to get us some ice cream from the store around the corner. He never came back, not after one, not after two days.

When he finally returned, he was brought back by the police. On his way to the ice cream parlor a car with a few black girls had offered to give him a ride. There was no need for him to get any ride, but the attraction of all these girls was too great than and he could not resist the offer. Where did they take him? To Belle Isle, the island in the Detroit River, near where we lived. It turned out that these girls were all part of a black female motor cycle gang. Once they had him in their power, they threatened him at gun point, pulling off his clothes and trying to gang rape him.

The fact that Dawud could not be scared by anything or anyone, took the fun away for them. They put him out at night without his clothes and so he was found by police wandering the streets of Detroit. They took him to the police station and to a hospital. Finally after two whole days Dawud arrived back home.

I wanted to write this book to start to understand the riddle of this person and my connection with him. Rudolf Steiner asked of Waldorf teachers* to make the effort of solving the riddle of each child in their classes "from day to day, from hour to hour". In addition to trying to solve the riddles of the children I worked with in my professional life, I so much wanted to understand Dawud and where he was coming from.

Durkheim, a famous French Sociologist, Criminologist (1858-1917) warned us: "In order that the originality of the idealist whose dreams transcend this century may find expression, it is necessary that the originality of the criminal, who is below the level of his time, shall also be possible. One does not occur without the other."

People react very differently on difficult and abusing home situations. Some just somehow suffer and go along with it, others react by becoming mentally or physically ill, some smart people like Dawud react with deep disdain for the world. They are going to take their anger and frustrations out onto the world.

<u>Searching for the Real Dawud</u>

In my imagination all of this was not the real Dawud. I had gotten to know by now two sides of him: the one who could write about Unicorns and do all the other cultural activities, and the one who was now "free" but still had to learn how to deal with life in the "free" world. One night he came home with a chain for a weapon in his hands, all worked up, because the boy friend of a girl he had visited was coming after him. I kept the wholesome picture of Dawud in my heart over and over again. After all these and other adventures Dawud always had a place to come home to, which was most important. Because of the fact that he could not get any work in Michigan, after some months I suggested to him that we should try to go to Texas, where I had connections as a result of having been there on two occasions to give Eurythmy workshops at Waldorf and Anthroposophical conferences. One of these people I had gotten to know in College Station told me that she knew of a house on a ranch that we could rent for $ 50 a month!

Texas on the Ranch

While Michigan was suffering from a high unemployment rate, Texas had an oil boom. It still was a miracle that Dawud got a job to work at an oil rig. A few days earlier someone at the top of the derrick had accidentally dropped a hammer which had killed the worker who was working down below. People hesitate and see it as a bad omen and would rather not take the place of someone who had just died from an accident. It was Dawud's good luck that they were willing to give the job of that worker to him. The newcomer has of course to do the most dirty jobs like fishing tools out of the oily grime. They did not just fall in there. They were thrown in on purpose to test the newcomer. From then onward Dawud would come home every evening in oil drenched clothing. There was no way you could wash these clean and get rid of the oil smell. So I went regularly to the thrift shop to get him new sets of clothes, including underwear.

It wasn't in any kind of way fulfilling for Dawud, so he might come home tired, dismayed and angry about things that happened that day. One day, when I, unwittingly, said something he did not like, he pushed the whole round table, with all the food and dishes on it, over. If this had happened at home with his mother and step father, they would have created an uproar, feeding the emotional upheaval to a record high. The only things I said was "You better get a broom and tidy up the mess" which he did. This was the only time he ever did this, as there, obviously, wasn't much emotional coinage he could get out of this.

Dawud never ever had a place like this on his own. The house was old and sloping. Those who left in a hurry had luckily left all the furniture. This was good as we only had what we could carry in the car with which we drove down from Michigan. Dawud anyway had so little. Besides personal clothing, I only brought my books and notes to be able to continue my work as a Eurythmist. I was happy to get two days of work at the Austin Waldorf School. That meant that I would be two days a week away. It probably would have been better if I could have stayed at home. The reader may imagine that Dawud was starved for any female attention. With his good looks and inviting attitude he made friends quickly. He was like a bee in a honey jar. So I had to deal with his escapades, which sometimes resulted in a girl becoming pregnant.

One day he came home with a big painting in a gilded frame. He proudly searched for a spot where to hang it.

I didn't get much of an answer out of him as to where he had gotten it. I did not know that there are libraries that not only check out books, but also check out paintings. Dawud's idea of borrowing was not the usual one. He had no intention of bringing it back. Meanwhile, he already had a new adventure in bringing home two black puppy dogs, which he told me he had rescued from being drowned. He did the rescuing. From that time onward, I had the responsibility to take care of them.

As I said already on the first page with the example of Alabama Slim: Prison robs any inmate from ever having to take responsibility. What an indictment! It would take Dawud many years slowly to build up this feeling of responsibility. I was there for him as much as I could be. But someone else had an eye on him and pursued him relentlessly. She postured for a while as his cousin. Meanwhile her influence on him was so strong that, one day, he walked up to me, carrying the Koran under his arm, and declared: "It is written in the Koran that I as a man have the power to annul this marriage as of this moment. I declare hereby that we are divorced". No further commentary or questions were asked. We married in 1980. The divorce came at the beginning of 1983. Already in April 1983, Dawud remarried into what was going to be a stormy relationship. He and Tracy had one daughter together. I did not want to stay in College Station. Other Eurythmy work had presented itself round the whole of Texas and especially in Houston and Dallas. So I moved to Houston. Again I was given a whole inventory of furniture and whatever I needed in my new apartment. Little did I know that Dawud lived not too far away from me. It was strange to drive on the freeway and all of a sudden pass a car driven by Dawud. In that episode I still saw him a few times when he took care of the little baby. He wanted to be the best father he could possibly be and his new wife would later acknowledge that, indeed, he had been a very good father.

Being in Houston, Dawud had greater opportunities for work. He was most interested in the restaurant business and managed to move up through different restaurants, always acquiring new skills until, in 1984, he got a degree in Culinary Arts from the Houston Community College. Then the road was open to move from being a Line Cook to becoming a Banquet Chef and ultimately an Executive Chef in some of the most prestigious restaurants in Houston. One can say, he made the most out of the move, yet—as time will tell—had not yet shed his craving for drugs or some of his criminal mentality

Waiting without any Sign of Life

I had moved to Texas because of Dawud. There was no further reason for me to stay there much longer. I reviewed my years in the US: South Haven, Michigan, which gave me the chance to teach Eurythmy to Honor students at Michigan State University, the building up of a Eurythmy Center in Kalamazoo, teaching positions in Chicago and Detroit. While the red thread of my professional life continued unbroken, I still worked as much as I could with black children in schools, in day schools for the handicapped, in summer camps in the big cities of Detroit and Chicago.

Big cities have great cultural advantages but mostly also are breeding places for crime. In a timeslot of the ten years in America, I had had a lot of exposure to street crime. It wasn't just my connection with a career criminal. Twice my house was burglarized, once in Kalamazoo and once in Detroit. Each time the invaders cleared me out thoroughly. At other times the petrol of my car was siphoned off. Next I had to drive with a lock on the hood because people had stolen my battery. At one time in Detroit I went outside to go some place with my car, but the car had vanished overnight. Walking in the dark at night, I was taught to always keep one hand in my pocket so people would think that I had my hand on a gun. Miraculously, I have never been harmed personally. I always felt myself to be in the protection of the Archangel Michael*. There were times when I had to struggle on my chosen, but lonely path. But I always knew one thing: "I am in the service of the Archangel Michael." Even though unfortunate things happened to me, I still was positive about America and what I experienced as the greater spontaneity of the people and more freedom for private initiatives than in Europe.

Social Streak

As much as this book is an effort to understand the real being of Dawud and his intentions for this life time, it also helps to clear up things for myself.

What is this social streak in me? I am Dutch and know that Dutch people are mostly looked at as being socially minded. But there is more to this. During my Eurythmy studies, when I was 27, I had to undergo an operation in my throat, which was not supposed to be something too serious and could be done under local anaesthetics. Not being accustomed to using allopathic drugs, this had more of an impact than the doctor expected. The result was that I flipped out in the middle of the operation and looked at myself from high above, as I was lying there on the operation table. The doctor, the anaesthetist and the nurses were in a frenzy to bring me back to life. *Meanwhile, I was told "up there" that I was given the choice to either go back into my body or opt out.* What really influenced my decision more than anything else was the loving attention I received from one of the nurses. "If there are caring people like this, I should be among them", must have been my higher reasoning. After one has said "Yes" to life in such a positive way, one can never complain about life being too hard. It was my own choice, wanting to be here. By talking in later years to other people who have had similar near-death experiences, it dawned on me that my "social streak" had its origin in this Yes-to-Life attitude. People were people, young or old, independent of their social or cultural status, their state of health or ill-health, independent of belonging to the so-called free people or to the many people, being kept behind bars.

It's amazing that I am writing about all the bad things which happened to me in the Midwest. At the same time I was aware of the fact that it was also an area of great strength and character. After I had lived already a few years in Kalamazoo, I heard that Rudolf Steiner had mentioned Kalamazoo. Rudolf Steiner had never come personally to America, yet he made once this statement: "When I hold a series of lectures in Dornach, I do it in a certain way. If I would do this in Kalamazoo, I would have to do it in a totally different way." Thanks to his clairvoyant capacities, Rudolf Steiner was able to see the significance of this place which used to be an important center of Native American activity and had a central place as several trading routes merged in that area. By the way, the name Kalamazoo stands for Hot Springs. It was the place where I have felt most at home out of all the places where I have ever lived.

Chapter Four

Dealing with the Facts of Life

As my time in America wound down, I was pleased to get an offer to teach Eurythmy in South Africa. This had been a dream of mine to go one day to Africa. Over the years I had read every book written by Laurens van der Post*, especially his books about the Bushmen and the Kalahari Desert. I was in awe of this man who went out of his way to befriend some of the original Bushmen, who basically had been made outcasts of society. He showed us their innocence and their culture through his writing but also through the documentary, "The Lost World of the Kalahari". Just as in America where I worked intensively with black people, I now was keen to meet them in their land of origin.

Just before leaving the US for South Africa I had my last incident with street crime. I was visiting with friends in Detroit and wanted to take a letter to the mail box. As I walked across a busy street I noticed a man crossing from the other side. From afar I saw the glint in his eye and knew that he was up to no good. As he got near me—amidst all these people—he tried to jerk my purse from my shoulder. But I managed to fling the purse away. I hoped that it would land on the other side of a wall, but as it didn't, he ran and grabbed it. Immediately two policemen pursued him, but I had to notice that the motivation of the criminal was much greater than that of the pursuing officers. This was the first time here in America that someone robbed me in broad daylight. It made it all the more awkward as so many people were around, seeing what was happening, but doing nothing.

In South Africa I had to realize that it was still the dark time of Apartheid. I was not interested in going there in order to start living the good life of the whites. I only went because I knew that the director of the Waldorf School in Pretoria had offered the principal of a black farm school to resettle his school on the property of the Waldorf school. It was still out of the question and prohibited by law to educate black and white children together. So my work was going to be to teach three days of Eurythmy in the white school and two days in the black farm school. It was an exciting new beginning, yet ultimately not satisfying because of the Apartheid politics. We could not educate the children together. That was against the law. The whole situation affected me even more because I felt terrible that the people, promoting the Apartheid, were originally my countryman. I felt a Karmic obligation to represent the other side of the Dutch character, which is 'extreme tolerance", the opposite of racism.

Starting the Centre for the Art of Living in Africa

Soon a situation presented itself, enabling me with other friends from the Anthroposophical and Waldorf community in Johannesburg, to start a social venture which we called the Centre for the Art of Living. It had to do with trying to bridge the social divide between the blacks and the whites. Even though this was illegal, one of our first actions in 1985 was to bring black and white children together in a Christmas Holiday Camp. I have written about these experiences in my book Courage and Love for Children in South Africa*.

Apartheid was something abhorrent to me. My work would have to be to build bridges between the different factions of South African Society. This meant going to the places where the black population resided, where they were forced to live away from the white areas. The parents of the children, who were mostly from Soweto, in our first Holiday Camp, which took place during the 2-weeks Christmas break in 1985, wanted more for their children. Now that they had heard about Waldorf education, they could not think of anything better to benefit their children. After much preparation and earning the confidence of the black people, by convincing them that we were not fly-by-nights, we were able to start our first Waldorf Kindergarten in Alexandra, Johannesburg. Twenty-one years later this is still a thriving Waldorf school with some 360 pupils, going from strength to strength. This is all the more remarkable as Alexandra is one big slum, nearest to a most wealthy business district. Alexandra holds half a million people in one square mile. The unemployment rate is well above 70%. The place is drug-infested and has a very high crime rate. We trained the teachers ourselves, most of whom are still working in the school. They know what it means for the children and their parents that there is this haven of peace

Even though it was dangerous, the work was so engaging and promising that I did not have much time to think about Dawud. I was convinced that I had lost track of him and had surrendered to the idea that I might only meet with him again in the next life. Africa was an exciting new experience, not to be compared in any way with the Western way of life. I was in charge of a group of eighteen doll makers who worked on the grounds of the school. These women were parents of the school who were able to earn a little bit of income from the sales of the dolls. Of the eighteen women, a few had come as far as attending fourth or fifth grade, but most of them were illiterate. My communication with them had to proceed with the help of interpreters as they all came from different tribes and knew no English. These women, who had grown up in the rural areas, still were connected with their cultural heritage. They were an important link for us to create a Waldorf school in a black township—the first one ever— that wasn't a replica of a German Waldorf school but would embrace Africa in a deeper way.

Crime in Africa

Yet, it was at the same time dangerous to work there. There were not only the purse snatchers, the break-in artists, but many black people in the township had already embraced organized crime. When a car was stolen, within half an hour that car would have been totally dismantled or have found its way already in the direction of the borders. It happened twice to me that the car was hi-jacked while I was in it. The first time by four guys at gun point, the second time by one man who wielded a knife. I and my passengers came away unscathed, but each time we lost the car and important documents. As I meditated later in the day about the first incident, I felt how the man, who I had seen close-up eye to eye, came into my orbit but as a little baby who only wanted to be held by me. As in the dealing with crime and criminals in America, here too one needed to understand the reasons why people come to these desperate acts. Coming to this insight, helped me to get over the shock.

We had the opportunity of meeting directly with inmates in prisons in Johannesburg. We offered to perform a Paradise and a Christmas Play for the inmates of the prison, which we had already performed for the Waldorf school community and other groups in Johannesburg. People at that time in South Africa might be in prison for serious crimes but could also have been picked up because they had stolen a loaf of bread. The prisons we went to were supposed to be model prisons to show how well blacks were treated. It was quite an experience to play for 1600 men all at once. The second time we did our Christmas play in an open court yard under the blazing sunshine. Many prisoners came forward to thank us and to comment on the content of the plays. Later on we heard that the inmates had started to perform their own play, a play in which all the roles including Mary and the angel were played by men.

Receiving a Letter from Dawud

And then, what I had expected the least, happened. I lived together with my dear friend Claartje. We had a very harmonious relationship. Anyone, who saw us together, was convinced that we must be sisters. My friend and I were both sure that, indeed, we had been sisters but then in another life time. Our work with the black people was intensive and fulfilling. One day in 1989 a letter from Dawud arrived. Was I reluctant to open it? I can't remember. But once I opened it and read the contents, I was floored. Dawud was back in prison.

He had gone out of his way to get my address in South Africa. It took him three and a half years, while leaving no stone unturned, to find out about my whereabouts. Even though I don't easily cry, I never cried so much in my life as I did that day when I received his letter. I just could not stop crying. And even when I got over that, I was not myself for a whole week. What was I going to do with that letter? I told myself that I could not act as if I never received it. It had too much of an impact on me. After an interruption of five years I started corresponding with him again.

Dawud told me in his letters that he had done very well professionally, earned very good money and was always looking to improve his position. Then, in 1986, after only three years he and his wife divorced. He had felt very lonely since that time and fell back into his old habit of using cocaine. While working as a chef in a prestigious yacht club, he took off one day—in the stupor of a super dose—with the total earnings of the day. It did not take the police too long to find him. They arrested him in New Orleans while in possession of a fire arm. While waiting in jail he prayed fervently that they would not have access to his whole criminal records. This is exactly what happened. Through a 'glitch' in their computer system they did not link this happening with any information from his old criminal records. As a result he only received a 6-months sentence for something which they considered to be a "misdemeanor".

Sexual Assault Charge

Dawud was released after having served just six months in prison. He went back to his former wife. They were legally divorced but still lived for a while together. Meanwhile his former wife had met someone else she had fallen in love with. It is in this time, in 1988 that Dawud came down with a new and very serious charge: one of sexual assault against his ex-wife. Her story to the police obviously had a much bigger impact than what Dawud had to say about it. She greatly embellished the story by telling the police that he had tried to murder her and that the whole assault had taken place in front of their little daughter. Being coerced to plead guilty, Dawud agreed with the fact that he forced her to have sex, while denying vehemently the other embellishments of the story.

In a Maximum Security Prison

This is what Dawud had to say about it in his letter to me:

"Damn, damn, damn! It is really beyond explanation as to how terribly ashamed I am to find myself in this pathetic, sorry-ass situation once again. My spirits (what's still left of them) have never been so bleak and forlorn. It would be easy to think that I could just do away with my stupid and wasted life, but be assured, I am not a coward or a quitter. What is the worst right now is that I will not be able to see my daughter. Her mother will not under any circumstances bring her to see me. I miss her so much, it's like a real physical pain that's with me continuously twenty-four hours a day. She will be six soon. It is three a.m., the only time it is quiet in this place, and I can feel your presence so close as though you were sitting on the other side of my desk—staring at me—with this sort of questionable expression in those mysterious brown eyes. I imagine you are asking: "When are you going to get your life together and do something meaningful for yourself and the world?" I wish I could answer that question or even discuss the pros and cons of it more in depth with you, but at the moment I am too preoccupied with plain survival to be concerned with just about anything else. But then again, under the circumstances, I believe that the example I try to set every day is in itself a contribution."

"You wanted to know the difference between this place and Jackson prison. They are light years and dimensions apart. This is a real prison. It makes Jackson in comparison seem like Disney Land. Another way to put it is to say that it is the Alcatraz of the Texas Prison System. Which means that out of the 40,000 inmates incarcerated in the State of Texas, they have systematically screened out the worst of the worse and sent them here. They have got some real live monsters running around masquerading as human beings, and I am talking about 80 to 85% of the population. It is like they're totally void of any sense of personable integrity or moral character. It's a weird, sick, perverted man-made hell!! I've been here two years and it's been the longest most repugnant two years of my entire life."

Spiritual Nourishment

There were also some bright lights in Dawud's gloomy situation. In a letter to me of that time he is happy to report that he received a package together with a very cordial letter from the Anthroposophical Prison Outreach*. "Very rarely do I have the opportunity to read something that alters my pattern of thinking and also expands my consciousness. There was a passage in the book "The Beneficent Role of Destiny" that touched me deeply: Instead of blaming others for our painful experiences, we should say to ourselves in the depths of our souls that we ourselves have been the cause of all such things. It is we ourselves who caused something to happen to us as recompense for something we have done. And thus do we come to a right attitude toward our life, to a broadening of our perspectives, when we say: "Everything that befalls us comes from ourselves. Our own action is fulfilled outwardly even when it seems as if someone else performed it". I took that book to my Narcotic Anonymous group meeting and read portions of it to the other members. Needless to say, the response was truly remarkable!"

"I know that my self-centeredness has for too long stunted my spiritual growth. Remember, I have come a long way. Even though I was brought up catholic, I totally lost my faith. I became an agnostic, or stronger, an atheist. I only joined the Muslim community in Jackson prison because I was so emotionally starved and hungered for companionship. I am reading your letters over and over and over. They are my life line. I am also deeply engrossed in other Steiner books, but I have to digest his meditations very slowly as his level of consciousness is so high. It is actually so awesome that I can only read one or two paragraphs a day." When I sent him Rudolf Steiner's Foundation Stone Verse*, his reaction was: "It is too deep to get it straightaway, so I just repeat it a hundred times in one instance." Finally, Dawud comes to this conclusion: "I understand now how important it is to affirm one's own destiny. In this way we forge an Ego that does not break down when incomprehensible things happen. An Ego that endures, that endures the truth and that is capable of coping with the world and with fate. Then, to experience defeat is also to experience victory. Nothing is disturbed—neither inwardly nor outwardly—for one's own continuity has withstood the current of life and of time."

Carlos the Caterpillar*

In this time Dawud was even capable of writing a beautiful children's story while living under those most challenging and dangerous conditions. The high level of constant loud noises, the blaring TV's, the screaming of commands of guards and of prisoners from cell to cell, the metal doors being slammed, the clanging of keys when turned to lock the cell doors, it all was impacting on one's sanity. The noise level was ongoing. Only late at night it finally would die down. That is when Dawud came to life and did his writing.

The story of Carlos the Caterpillar, who hopes one day to become a beautiful Monarch butterfly, can almost be understood as an autobiographical story of Dawud's own life and his deepest wish to go through the same metamorphosis as Carlos. This in short is the story line, which—I regret to say—corrupts the beauty and intention of the story as one has to read the story in its entirety* to enjoy all the subtleties of his imaginative language, the freshness of the nature descriptions. This is all the more astounding when one realizes that the author is living in a concrete bunker, far removed from beautiful natural surroundings.

On a bright and clear summer morning Carlos is rescued from certain death by a dragonfly by the name of Nathaniel. It turns out that Nathaniel is a Knight of the Forest and that it is his sworn duty to protect all living beings and to defend the laws of nature. Now Carlos wants to know how

he could ever become a Knight of the Forest. Nathaniel gives him at first some very difficult tasks which Carlos is to master with courage and perseverance. He tells him what it would take to become a Knight of the Forest. "You should know that a knight is a defender of the small, the weak and the helpless, even if he's to put his own life into harm's way. Finally, a knight is always helpful to those in need, loyal to his friends, and truthful in all matters entrusted to him." After he has shown his worth,

Nathaniel takes him on as his squire and, in this capacity, Carlos, in turn, is able to rescue Nathaniel when he is on a very dangerous mission on behalf of the Queen of the Bees. Carlos, who manages all the tasks given to him with utter devotion, develops very quickly into a special squire, worthy of becoming a Knight of the Forest. But there is another beautiful part of the story when all the animals of the forest come together and the Council of Seven Knights comes to the important decision . . . . In one of his letters Dawud wrote: "Carlos has become a very elusive Butterfly, as I am having great difficulties ending the final chapter." Writing this book was his focal point for quite a while. Maybe he was hesitant to say good-bye to Carlos.

I tried to have the story published. I found a German children's book illustrator, who—according to my taste— made some wonderful illustrations for the book. She did this without any remuneration, as a gift to Dawud and me. I was sad that Dawud did not like the pictures as I did, but that he had something totally different in mind. Some time later he found an artist in prison, who created some amazing pictures, but quite different from the ones done by the German artist. Just before this person could do the last drawing, he was transferred to another prison. Again the efforts to get the book illustrated were thwarted. Before going for a visit to Europe I translated the story into German and also into Dutch. Many people have wondered: "Is this a story for children?" Dawud had in mind that it was perfectly allright for children from 9 years onward. Other people think that it should only be read by adults. There is also a problem with the publishers. Some tell us, it is too short for a reading book for older children. Others say, there is too much text and there are not enough illustrations to make it a picture book for smaller children.

I personally believe that it should be seen and experienced for what it is: a story of transformation, a path to nobility of character through service, written by someone whose deepest desire is to make those transformations himself. To write this under those harrowing circumstances should make it into a document of special interest. Dawud wishes the book to be recognized for its own literary merits.

First Visit after the Long Separation

Dawud kept asking me in his letters: "When are you able to come and see me?" That was not so easy to do as I was now living thousands of miles away in South Africa. Finally in November 1992, I was able to book a flight to the US. Dawud was now in a different location in Texas, in Dallas, where I did not know any people. This meant that I had to book a motel and rent a car. I already said earlier that the prisons are always far away from the urban centers. I managed to make all those preparations and found the prison. But then something happened that I never had felt before in my relation to Dawud. I saw that huge concrete fortress with the guard towers and the electrified barbed wire fences, and, as I stood there, I got so angry. "How did you manage this again to get yourself once more incarcerated behind prison walls. You are so smart and yet . . . !" I had to get over this sudden burst of anger, get myself into a conciliatory mood before I could enter the prison. Entering the prison complex sounds simple, but also has its challenges. Actually, one's car is thoroughly searched for weapons before entering the grounds. I had been sent away at the gate on other occasions as my passport did not have the same first name as the driver's license (Geertruida versus the abbreviated version of Truus). Or you have to wait hours in the rain, because so many people come to visit. Visits are only on weekends. I still was not sure if they would allow me a contact visit, which means one hug at the beginning and one hug at the end. In between you can sit together at a table inside or outside with four feet of table space in between inmate and visitor. Well, this privilege was not granted me—or I should say us—because we would have to talk by telephone while looking over a frosted glass window. When Dawud finally showed up, we said that this set-back was not going to spoil our visit. Because I came from afar and Dawud never had any other visitors, we were allowed four hours each time over two consecutive days. Dawud would always say: "With you I never get bored. I can talk with you for ever." And so it was. At the end of the second day, we had to say good-bye, not knowing when we might see each other again as I had still strong commitments in South Africa.

Getting Remarried?

Quite soon after this visit Dawud started talking in his letters about getting remarried. He had experienced first hand what it means when your partner all of a sudden leaves you for someone else. He realized what he had put me through. He sent me a most touching piece of writing, which he called 'Favorite One'.

"Twenty years ago when you found me wandering in the forest of my discontent, your light was much too bright for me to see who you really were. Even though I can close my eyes and recall every explicit detail of that first encounter, as if it just occurred this morning. For far, far too long I remained deaf, dumb and blind to the marvelous being that had descended into my life. I was deaf to your truth because I didn't always speak it. I was dumb as a stone to think that I could forsake your grace and not suffer the consequence, because karma will always reap karma, but above everything else, I was blind to an uncommon loyalty that knew no bounds."

After my first experience I was not so quickly swayed this time. Dawud was aware of that, so he kept at it repeatedly. I got the following story as a birthday present from him:

The Gypsy and the Wolf

After the music had stopped and the camp fire was just an afterglow, the Gypsy sat beneath a canopy of stars and stared at the amber eyes of a fearsome wolf in the shadows of the moonlight.

Her mind questioned why she had followed those eyes through too many storms of uncertainty, but her heart knew secrets that her dreams could not fathom.

When she was just a wee lass wandering in the Low Lands, an oracle, disguised as a raven, told her that she was destined to meet her heart's desire in a far-off distant land which the gods had forsaken.

"How will I know him?" she earnestly quired. "When the eleventh moon crosses into the sixth house you'll meet in a dungeon and your seasons will be more than his, but he'll be wise beyond his years."

"Will he love me?" she beseeched.

"He has loved you since stars were but cosmic dust whirling in ethereal space, and he will continue to love you until there is no more pulse in the universe.

And so it came to pass that she met her prince, and, for too short a while, they rejoiced in each other's song, but their karma was not to dance in fields of splendor beneath skies of milk and honey. Their roads would be filled with tragedy darkened with clouds of despair.

The odyssey began when they went camping deep in a northern forest. Under a luminous moon one night she performed eurythmy—which was her artistry—for the delight of her mate alone. Suddenly, a large and very fierce looking wolf appeared at the edge of the forest; whereupon he seated himself royally as if he had received a personal invitation.

Fearlessly she continued her performance without a moment of hesitance, but, while she whirled about majestically, all her Gypsy senses bespoke of something dramatic to happen, and it did. When she turned to smile at her love,r he had vanished!

Glancing back at the wolf they stared deeply and longingly into each other's eyes. She knew then where her heart had gone.

Dawud's poetic depth can also be read when he uses the word 'Low Lands'. This means of course the low lands of the Netherlands. And 'when the eleventh moon crosses into the sixth house", this relates to the fact that I was born—as was he—on the sixth day of the eleventh' month. This story, more than anything else, reveals the duality living in Dawud's soul.

I could respond only with another story:

The Princess and the Wolf

Once upon a time there was a princess who always had her eyes half-closed. People would come and ask her mother, the queen, if she was half a-sleep. "Oh no", the queen said, "She is very awake. By keeping her eyes half closed, she can observe the world much better. In fact, I know she is able to look through the surface of things."

But the princess was not always observing. She also loved to play wild games, whenever she had the chance. She was witty and awake and most of the time happy. One thing, however, she did not like. These were quarrels. There should be peace, she thought, why fight and feel unhappy?

One day when she had gone to her favorite place, the palace garden, and was looking with great interest at the bees and the butterflies, her eye fell on a white and furry animal, sitting on his hunches near the garden gate. "I am wild", said the beast, "I am a wolf. Don't come near me". "You can be wild if you want to", said the princess, "but I think you have come because you are lonely." At that the wolf leapt away, back into the forest. Now the princess became a little bit lonely too. She had to think about the words the wolf had spoken. She wondered where he was and why he did not show himself again.

When she had almost forgotten about the short encounter, she saw him again, this time just outside the garden gate, where she had gone to explore a bit the world beyond the safety of the palace. "You should not be here", said the wolf. "It is here that wild things happen." "How come you came back", asked the princess. "I am looking for company", said the wolf, "but everybody is afraid of me." "I am not" was the answer of the princess. "I think you are beautiful. You are just enchanted. Can you shed your wolf skin?" At that the wolf gave a terrible howl and disappeared in the distance.

Now in turn the princess was devastated. She started looking out for him every day. But she also had to attend to her lessons and all the special things that a princess must learn. The king and the queen also started to talk to her about finding a suitable man to marry. As time went on and the princess was not in the least interested in anyone her parents suggested, they started to pressure her into making a decision. In her despair she fled into her peaceful garden, where she could think and be all by herself.

She had not quite settled at a rock near the garden pond, when she heard a muffled sound behind her. As she turned her head, she saw her friend, the white wolf, coming towards her in big leaps and bounds. "I had to come back" he said, "You are the only one I want to be with." At that the princess reached out for her friend, who finally had come back to her. At the moment that she wanted to embrace him, the wolf skin tore open and fell away from him. The princess gasped as she had never seen such a shining knight. It seemed as if there was a sun inside him, which was radiating through his whole being and beaming from his face toward her. No words needed to be said. The enchantment was broken and they knew they would not be separated anymore.

Imagine the eyes of the king and the queen, when they presented themselves to them. This indeed was a wonder, unsurpassed by anything they had ever heard of. All they could do was to give their blessing to this beautiful pair, which seemed to know what they were doing and where they were going.

The story did not quite end here, because I found on the back of Dawud's expressive drawing of the wolf the following words:

Although the wolf has weathered
Many cold storms alone, he'll
Always remember the starry
Night you bravely invited his
Savage Heart to share the warmth
Of your fire.

What did you see in the wolf's
Eyes that night, which assured
You he wouldn't pounce and
Devour . . . . while you danced
Elegantly beneath the gypsy
Moon?

After he departed you did not
See him weeping in the forest
For having left the grace of
Your embrace.

Dawud wanted me so much to be back in his life, even though he had no idea when he might get out of prison. Talking about getting remarried, Dawud could be very persuasive. Did I feel any desire to get remarried? Not quite. Did I care about him? Very much so. I always kept before me the challenges he was facing day by day. He should tell now in his own words about the world he was surrounded by, and why he so desperately wanted to hold on to some security in the future.

The Day-to-Day Environment

"In this dog-eat-dog subculture, there's a pre-described code of conduct, which says that we're expected to act mean, rude and disrespectful towards each other. This moronic train of thought is to show the others that you're tough. Being "nice" to people is an open invitation to the wolfs and parasites that you're either weak, stupid or crazy, and it's guaranteed that you'll be used and abused to the absolute limit of your endurance because there's no mercy or sympathy in prison! However, whenever I do reach out to someone, it helps me maintain my humanity, because I know that if I don't make a conscious effort, I could lose it and not even know it."

In this context the following story is of importance:

"While we were in the shower, a complete stranger asked me: "Hey man, let me use your soap" I told him that I don't do that. Totally ignoring what I just told him, he then says: "But I just want to lather down." I told him: "I've been over here numerous times and I didn't have any free world soap myself." After that he gave me a dirty look. While we were getting dressed, I got to think about what just happened, also about how extremely rare you see genuine acts of kindness, so I went over and gave him my bar of soap and walked away. When I handed it to him he looked at me as if he was retarded, but I know—even though it only was a fifty-five cent bar of soap—he'll never forget what I did. The whole point of the matter is this: Whenever I do something as I've just described, it helps me to stay human myself."

Here are a few more realities, inmates need to deal with. Because of the overcrowding of the prisons, cells that were meant for *one* person, are now inhabited by *two*. It is like life in a submarine. You <u>have</u> to get along with each other. But when, as in Dawud's situation, you have to share your cell with a very sloppy, smelly person, who happened to call himself a 're-born Christian' and has to read the bible all day long aloud, it asks for a lot of restraint from the other person. Sometimes Dawud was lucky and a fruitful companionship ensued. In another prison Dawud shared a cell with an older black man, who had never learned to read and write. Dawud worked with him diligently every day and the result was that his cellmate was able to master the art of reading and writing. After his release he was able to write Dawud a letter in which he thanked him and told him that he can now read the newspaper and that life in a big way has changed for the better for him.

The other big thing in prison is that you are dependent on the moods of the guards who change every eight hours. "You are bossed around all day, like you are some kind of mongrel dog. I've never been able to understand why they feel it necessary to talk to us like we were a subspecies." Very soon Dawud decided that he was always going to answer every negativity positively. That needs inner work. When I asked Dawud what was the greater obstacle to deal with in prison, the inmates or the guards, he immediately answered: the guards. "Prison brings out the worst in those being kept, but also the worst in the keepers. They treat us with as much brutality, hatred and contempt as they can get away with. I've seen correctional officers of every rank and file commit crimes from petty theft to murder." The fact that every kind of drug, cigarettes or type of liquor can be bought for money in the prison, is because it is brought in by the guards who augment their income considerably that way.

Sources of His Inner Strength

I am on a never ending quest to try and get a deeper understanding of who this complex person I am "waiting for" really is. I already pointed to the fact that Dawud calls himself a self-centered person. I add to this that I call him a person who was desperately in need of self-realization. Even though he called himself at certain times in his life agnostic and an atheist, he is aware of the fact that his life has been spared mysteriously so many times, that he has been praying that the computer would have a glitch, so the police would not see his past criminal records. He likes to stress that he even prayed me into his life. He is aware that there is some protecting force in his life. It is a fact that so many of his contemporaries, young people with whom he grew up with, who were in the gangs with him, as well as people he got to know in prison, all died violent deaths. Dawud hardly has a scratch. *He knows somewhere in his being that he's been saved for a purpose.*

But praying did not always alter the course of actions in the long run. For a hard-core career criminal to change, many influences are necessary. He wrote at one time to me: "You are the only person that really understands who I am and what I am going through." My answer to this is that you have to love a person to really understand him, even if the outside world looks at you as if you have lost it. They say that love makes one blind. lovers live with the fact that they have a deep knowledge about the inner goodness of the other person.

It is interesting to look at Dawud's baby photos, the only ones still in existence. As small as he is, you can see he is a very willful child, a fighter and not easy to deal with. In his biographical sketch Dawud tells that he learned from me that "the greatest atrocity you can commit on your self is to tell a lie or break your word. Every time you do this, it weakens your will, and your will is the foundation of your being". Imagine the difference of my and his upbringing. My mother would rather bite her tongue than say anything she could not make true. Dawud's life, on the contrary, has been stunted from early on by empty promises.

The Big Turn-Around

In Dawud's own words: "The sentiment which sparked my renaissance, was the feeling I experienced one day of not wanting to hurt anyone, my family, society or myself, ever again." In the time that I, his partner, was still in South Africa and, after that subsequently three years in Maine, Dawud requested help from the resident psychologist of the prison, a Dr Quackenbush*. Dawud had come to a point in his life, when he had hit rock bottom, where he knew he wanted to make some real changes. At the same time he realized that he was in need of therapy. He requested to be given the possibility of having weekly counseling sessions with a psychologist. It came to pass that Dawud was given the chance of having regular sessions with Dr. Quackenbush, who immediately told him that he had a major advantage over all his other clients because he came to him *out of his own free choice*, whereas the Parole Board had recommended therapy for all the others who seek it. The weekly sessions meant a lot to Dawud and helped him to start reviewing his own thought and behavior patterns. It lasted for over four years.

Dawud did a lot of soul searching and came to the conclusion that he wanted more than anything else <u>to have absolute honor with himself.</u> "I quickly discovered that becoming an honorable man wasn't something that was going to happen overnight, as I still possessed some deep seated character flaws that I needed to curtail first."

I mostly managed to write to Dawud every week. He did so in return. That is why I have stacks of letters from him, about two feet high, but there is no letter left from me to him. Cells have very little private locker space, so he would read and reread and once again read each letter, but then dispose of it. At one time he tells: "The way you have treated me has had more of an impact, more of an influence on my life and way of thinking, than any other single factor I've ever experienced."

Chapter Five

<u>Dawud, Turning 50</u>

"When I turned fifty in '98, I had already been turned down by the Parole Board four times. I remember thinking that day (November 6) that I had spent my tenth birthday in Juvenile Hall, my twentieth in the Reformatory, my thirtieth in Jackson Prison, and my fortieth in the Michael's Unit. My pen isn't capable of describing the utter self-loathing I experienced on being in another Texas prison on my fiftieth birthday, except to say it was by far the darkest day of my entire life."

I have only one letter I wrote to Dawud, because I kept the draft of it.

"Dawud, my dear friend,

"Your heart is sore with sadness. You ask yourself: "What did I do, why me, what challenge to this incarnation by a force more powerful than me? What has the world come to that economics rules the world, my prison world? Growing up as a teenager I had a deep disdain—it's true—

because I detested what I saw around me. How could God allow a world development like this?"

"My choice was to bury the flame deep inside me, to harden my ego, to turn my back, to hurt the world that was hurting me. This place, where I am stuck, wants to dull the last zest for life that I still feel in me. Where is the Spirit of Christ, the total forgiveness as a latent potential in me? Where is the flame I buried so long ago? My moments of silence are utterly painful. Can I reach for that new beginning, for that place of sanity in an insane surrounding?

Is there HOPE, not only for me, but for the world as a whole?"

So far I tried to live myself into Dawud's situation. The rest of my letter to him came from a place of hope. "HOPE is a state of inner activity, a state of delicate balance, a face uplifted to the real powers at work. HOPE is the youngest force of the soul. Only Christ himself—the Spirit Sun—is capable of these revolutionizing changes which need to take place. I feel I am pregnant with Hope, just for the sake of it and for no other reason than to bring Hope to a new birth. Is that what the Spirit of Christmas tells us? Stay pregnant with Hope. Only the stars know the correct moment of birth."

Release and Parole Violation

The sexual assault charge would haunt Dawud for decades to come. All the rules dealing with that crime are more heavily enforced than with any other crime. Because he pleaded guilty, the time to serve was reduced to five years instead of the twenty five year sentence, which he would have to serve otherwise. After a while Tracy, his former wife, started corresponding again. She told him in a letter that she actually had forgiven him for the sexual assault. She made this statement once more in the form of an official Affidavit. The Parole Board took this Affidavit and mitigated his sentence. They paroled him in 1991 after only three years! While still on parole Dawud wrote a letter to his ex-wife, saying that he would not allow her to stay in his way to see his daughter. This was perceived as a threat and because of that his parole was revoked.

Just before that, while Dawud was without a penny and feeling miserable, he totally lost it when a lady stopped her car and asked him for directions. Instead of giving directions, Dawud took her purse and ran away with it. He had not been alone when this happened and his 'friend' told the police about it. As a result he received a new eighteen year sentence for Non-Aggravated Burglary of an Auto. By the way, the purse contained a mere $1.25. He would have to serve at least 50% of the eighteen years. That made him eligible for parole by August 2000. This time Dawud was only two and half months in the "free" world. In the years to come the Parole Board would turn him down several times.

Austin, Texas

Finally, in January 2002, after "serving" ten and a half years, Dawud was paroled to friends of mine in Austin, Texas. His troubles were not over yet, as the parole officer assigned to his case, made him sign papers, in which it was stipulated that he could not come within a distance of 30 feet from a place where children usually gathered. This was incorrect because there was nothing in Dawud's history that spoke of indecent behavior with children; on the contrary, his former wife had said that he had been a good father. If Dawud had not signed the papers, he would have been returned to prison immediately. It meant that Joanna and Larry, the friends who opened their home for him, had to put a lock on the room where they kept their computers, because Dawud "might otherwise look at porn". It also meant that they could never invite friends with children to their home. It made it practically impossible for Dawud to find work. Having a sexual assault charge on your records is bad enough, but having in addition restrictions involving minors, made it practically impossible to get work. He often was close to the possibility of being hired, but somehow there are always children around. Luckily he could do a lot for his hosts by working in the yard, cleaning house, and painting the kitchen. But he still had to go out every day to try and find a job. If you don't find a job, this is a reason to be sent back to prison.

Technical Parole Violation

Dawud had to wear an electronic monitor in form of an ankle band. This meant that he had to adhere to an absolute rigid schedule. Once a week, at the meeting with the Parole officer, the schedule for the whole week had to be finalized. It would cover shopping for groceries, going to the hairdresser, taking classes at the Parole Office for those charged with Sexual Assault. To get to any of the job interviews he had to take the bus, sometimes two buses. It was a totally nerve-racking time for Dawud, because the smallest deviation from the plan would already have put him back into prison. Often he had to resort to taking a taxi to be back "home" before the time on his schedule ran out. When I visited Dawud in Texas, I could use the car of my friends to get groceries. Dawud would be standing just inside the doorframe of the front door, but could not even do one step onto the outside doormat, to take the grocery bags from me.

By that time Dawud had already had 65 job interviews. Because he had to tell up front that he had been in prison for sexual assault, nobody would hire him. Being an accomplished chef and very able to present himself well, he was curious if he still was marketable, so he decided that on one occasion he would tell the owner of the restaurant only by his second visit that he had been in prison and for what reasons. This time they hired him, but the parole officer had already checked up on him and heard from the restaurant owner that he had not told them the full story of his incarceration. That was a serious parole violation. Another time Dawud had two job interviews on one day, which were rather close together. The stipulation on his schedule was to go to the first interview, take the bus to go home, then take another bus to go for the second interview. Dawud had a moment of unawareness and went from the first interview directly to the second one. This was another infraction on the rules, both of them seemingly minor.

Sex Offender Rehabilitation Program

Dawud had to attend weekly sessions in a Sex Offender Rehabilitation Program. Of the ten persons in the group, eight were convicted pedophiles. Dawud, who never had any dealings with minors in that sense, had to do all kinds of exercises where he had to speak up about his thoughts and feelings, about his reactions when he saw children, or even only pictures of children. When he tried to explain to the therapy worker that he believed that this was not the correct treatment for him, as nothing in his past history spoke of such a sexual orientation towards children, he was then judged as being in denial and not cooperative with the treatment program. From then onward the treatment provider and the female parole officer began a drive to drop him from the program. This would mean being returned to prison. This combined with the two minor parole violations brought Dawud down. He had the strong intuition that this was going to happen. Was he going to be sent back once again or was he going to elope and become an outlaw? Dawud fought an inner battle. And because he had made up his mind that he was never ever going to hurt anybody anymore, neither his family nor me, he let himself be incarcerated once again.

The charge was Technical Parole Violation. The prison time for that violation was supposed to be no longer than one year. But for Dawud, it turned into another four and a half yeasr.

Getting Remarried

The date for the wedding had been set for February 2, 2002. According to numerologists this should be a very special date. Indeed it was, because on this date Dawud was whisked off to jail and I had no partner to get married to. We had not planned anything bigger than just going through the official ceremony at the marriage license bureau and then, later in the day, having a little celebration with our hosts, Joanna and Larry. Now I had to ask Larry to substitute for Dawud and be my proxy. In my years with Dawud I had learned to live with disappointments. The "system" was always looming big over our connection. I thought of Dawud. Whisked away, again, again and for what? How would he be taking this new set-back? He had tried to comply as best as he could with all the rules, which was practically impossible.

When one is hooked to an electronic monitor 24 hours a day, that person's nervous system has to be on high alert all the time, not to make any mistake. Already the slightest mistake can be the reason for the parole to be revoked. As will be delved into in another chapter, more and more prisons were being built all over the United States but especially in Texas, which had to be filled to capacity with prisoners. How could this be achieved? By having judges hand out longer and longer sentences, by taking away 'good time' from inmates, and by returning ex-offenders to prison for the slightest infraction of the rules. The ones in charge and representing the "system" can also not be expected to act objectively. There clearly was a kind of agreement between Dawud's (female) parole officer and the treatment provider, to fill his rehabilitation class with as many ex-offenders as possible. Was this the reason that the parole officer classified Dawud as a pedophile, even though there was nothing in his past that should have warranted this? Nowadays many of the prison services are privatized. So was the Ex-offender Rehabilitation Class. Every person enrolled in that class had to pay $40 per class. Dawud did not have any paid work, so I paid for him. Being unable to pay for the class would already have been a reason to be put back into prison. Dawud was especially irked by the fact that in each class, he had to introduce himself with the words: "I am David Bullis, I am a pedophile", and then had to write each week extensively about his feelings when he saw a child, in a picture or in reality, about the kind of sexual desires this called up in him.

So I went on the arm of Larry through the motions of getting remarried I t was eerie. As soon as I could, I went to see Dawud in jail. Yes, here I was, newly married and talking through a telephone with my "husband" only as long as the time was allotted. Trying to cheer me up, he was still stunned, deprived once more of his freedom. The one good thing was that he could make phone calls as long a he wanted. These were our substitute for not being together. Little did I know then that these phone calls were a scheme to make money for the Department of Corrections, as the cost of any phone call was ten times more than in the free world. Especially when I wanted to talk with Dawud when I was already back in California, these phone calls cost me a fortune. As soon as they had him classified as a Technical Parole Violator, he was sent on to a facility for parole violators. Then the phone calls abruptly stopped, as the new situation did not allow again for any phone privileges

The "Holiday" Unit

After six weeks in jail, Dawud was shipped to a huge transit prison which is a holding place where people are kept until decisions are made as to their classification and where they ought to be, according to the system. Dawud described this unit as one of the most treacherous ones of the system. The good thing was that he could take college classes: Computer Maintenance and Computer Electronics. Taking college classes is for those who can pay for it. To me it was very important that Dawud was able to do something meaningful which in the end might enhance his possibilities for work, or just for self-employment, where you need that kind of skill. At this time Dawud was still under the assumption that he would only have to serve one year because of being a parole violator. After being there half a year he found out that he would be transferred once more.

Shipped Again

Yes, he was shipped again and this time to a huge prison complex, called the Hightower Unit. It is located in a far away rural place in East Texas and has forty dormitories of fifty inmates each. Dawud spent all his time there in one such dormitory with fifty inmates all day every day. There were about three television sets, all competing in sound intensity. There were fights quite regularly. It was going on towards summer and already very hot, into the nineties. The guards were in their air-conditioned spaces and would only come out if someone were unruly. Unruly could mean, taking off your shirt or putting a towel over your chair. The chairs were plain metal, which can be painful if you have to sit on them all day long. It would have helped if people could have used their towels to cushion the chairs, but that also was not allowed. Sometimes there was 'lock-down', which meant that all the inmates had to stay days on end on their bunk beds. When the restrictions were lifted again, Dawud would talk to some of the younger inmates about finding a way out of this deadly spiral of drugs and incarceration.

Then Dawud did something remarkable, daring, I should say. At 11:00 pm after the lights were off and quiet had returned, he got up from his bunk bed. Standing next to it, he started to recite the Lord's Prayer. Quite a few of the inmates came to him the next day to thank him for doing this.

Writing His Autobiographical Sketch*

At some point I asked Dawud to start thinking about writing his biography, at least a short version of it. Imagine the concentration it needs to work under such circumstances. On the other hand, the only way to survive the madness is to do something meaningful. He complied with my request and managed to write a little bit every day. Dawud gave this biographical sketch the title "How Can You Win, If You Are Not Right Within." It is remarkable the kind of objectivity he displays in telling his own harrowing story: his youth, full of abuse and without any guidance. Then he became a gang banger and spent months in Juvenile Hall with nightly physical abuse from an attendant. His experiences in the Reformatory resulted in his becoming much more criminally minded and violent. The gift of destiny was his discovery of the classics and his becoming totally absorbed in them. Finally, he came to Jackson Prison where I met Dawud after he had been there already nine years. The contents of his biography were so gripping that the editor of New View in England, who read the story while on the plane to the "continent", said to himself: "This is a must for our readers". Quite a few readers gave their feedback. They were very impressed and touched by it. Europe is still baffled about the way America deals with crime and punishment. They know that the US has totally given up on the idea that there should be something like rehabilitation. Imprisonment here has just become an economic issue. After Dawud's autobiographical Sketch found such an echo in England, I started to translate his story into German and Dutch. Some time later Dawud's life story appeared almost unabridged in the German magazine Info-3. By that time, I had already added my part of the story which I called "Trying To Win in a No-Win Situation". That's how I experienced the hopelessness of dealing with the Criminal Justice System.

Over the years I had engaged myself in Dawud's behalf in endless petitions and letters to officials. Those letters were mostly first conceived by Dawud because he knew better than anyone else the exact circumstances. The answers one would get, if any, were always stereotypes like: "We have put your letter in your husband's file."

Finally in 2006, after **four** *years of being incorrectly classified as a pedophile*, after I had paid much money for another lawyer and also our lawyer friend in San Antonio had tried to achieve something, Dawud got the letter we had been waiting for. It was from the Assistant Director of the Texas Department of Criminal Justice, who stated: "The child safety zone was <u>incorrectly</u> applied on Dawud's last parole". This was the message, no apologies whatsoever. Dawud was still in prison for this unholy mistake which brought so much hardship to both of us. He knew when he had to sign the papers at his release in 2002 that the classification of pedophilia was incorrect, but any objection and unwillingness to sign, would have put him straight back into prison then and there.

More Waiting from Truus' Perspective

While Dawud had his unending troubles, I was still unsure about my status in the US. I had paid a lawyer $6000 to obtain Permanent Residence Status but had great difficulty finding a sponsor. Of course, there is a risk involved for sponsors. If I should fall ill or have an accident the US Government would hold them responsible for my situation.

Just in the last week before the allotted time was up and I would have to return to Europe, I found a friend willing to sponsor me. Finally, in March of 2007, I received my Permanent Residence Card. I could stay in America. Only then did I feel free to start looking for a permanent place to live. I had lived for one and a half years in a tiny little room adjacent to a garage in the back yard of friends, where I had to do my cooking outside in the hot sun on an electric burner. I was most grateful for this opportunity but also happy that I could finally take all my furniture and books out of storage and could start looking for a regular apartment.

Dawud's Positive Reaction to Another Set-back

All along Dawud expected to be released after a year, as that used to be the usual time, meted out for a Technical Parole Violation. Shortly before the year was up, Dawud received information that he had to take a Sex Offenders Class for at least half a year. The real problem was that no openings were available to take this class. Once a place was available he had to be shipped to yet another prison where these special classes were held. Now instead of "serving one year" it could be anywhere between three to four years.

In total, Dawud was locked up for the technical parole violation from February 2002 till September 2007. How does one, time and again, overcome each of these monstrous set-backs? Dawud still had a lot of support, but many inmates have nobody in the free world, never receive any mail, and have no pocket money for the most necessary items. Dawud turned his deep frustrations around by starting to work intensively on an idea of how he could help first offenders to find a new direction and learn to step out of the vicious circle of going in and out of prison. He called it "Change, Instead of Chains".

Chapter Six

No Man is an Island

No man is an island. As much as Dawud, for safety's sake, had to keep distance to most of the prison population, he still was always able to find some friends, who were somehow compatible and with whom he could discuss and debate issues that were on his and their minds. Also the younger inmates flocked to him, some of them hanging on to his every word. He shared with them his life's experiences and how not to go the same path he went. One of the things Dawud did to keep his mind sharp was playing chess. He honed his skills with chess considerably over the years. Playing chess was a good pastime. Yet, whatever connections he made, no comradeship could endure for very long as sudden transfers could always be expected. Not only that people could be transferred to other prisons or released on parole. It could also happen that somebody would die in prison.

During this time that Dawud got very interested in Buddhism. "With absolute certainty, I know now what drew me to Buddhism more than anything else. It was because the core of it is not to harm, hurt or abuse any sentient being in any capacity, and to dedicate your life to becoming more enlightened." This conviction made it impossible for Dawud to kill evena cockroach. The consequence was that Dawud had more cockroaches in his cell than the neighboring cells. He just lets them be.

Eulogy for a Good Friend

It so happened that, shortly before his release, a very good friend of Dawud died in prison. Since people were aware of Dawud's close connection with Mason "Buzz" Johnson, the prison authorities asked him to speak the Eulogy at the funeral. I add it in its entirety to give not only an impression about this special man he so admired, but also to give a picture of Dawud and his writing skills.

"Last night I sat up into the wee hours of the morning trying to formulate and/or capture the proper words to express what kind of a person this Mason "Buzz" Johnson really was. Just to say that he was a good guy or that he was good people, would not be a befitting description, because in the entire length of time that I was privileged to have him as a close friend and confidant, I never knew him to step back from his principles. That, more than anything else was a true testament of his character, and a shining example for all of us to follow.

There was nothing fake or shallow about him, nor did he have any tolerance for the shuck and jive type either. If you weren't straight-up or on the for-real side, he had no reservations about telling you to get somewhere.

Besides his honesty and integrity, one of the things that I greatly respected and admired about him was his love for his people and his heritage, which was frequently displayed in his art work. Before his demise, he was working on a series of paintings entitled: "Back to Basics" which was centered around the unity and respect he felt was diminishing in the African American culture, and why there needed to be a revival of these basic ethics taught by our ancestors.

I know for a fact that he literally despised all forms of pretentiousness, especially liars and hypocrites. He also hated racism and injustice, not just the racism and injustice which has been prosecuted against his people, but all forms throughout the world.

In the truest sense of the word, Mason "Buzz" Johnson was a warrior. That's not to say he was anything like the African warrior inaccurately portrayed in the cinema of Hollywood. I mean he was a true warrior of just principles, devoted to the up-lift-ment of his people.

He was much, much more than just a friend to me, he was family, and for the rest of my life I'll carry with me a deep sense of reverence for his quiet dignity and indomitable spirit.

In essence, he was a Man's Man, who believed in doing the right thing just for the sake of doing the right thing.

If I had to describe him in just one word, it would be RIGHTEOUS."

In later years, as time went by, Dawud was more and more seen as a peacemaker in the prison. There were always some guards, who were able to keep to their own humanity and with whom Dawud could be on a cordial footing. Word had gotten around that Dawud was the kind of wordsmith who could not only write eulogies but also marriage vows. Some of the female guards, who were getting married were quite happy to pay him for whatever he could conjure up. Here is one such example:

Marriage Vows for a Female Guard

"I stand here before you today not only pledging my love and loyalty . . . but also my honesty in all matters of the heart.

We are about to embark on what could very well be the greatest adventure of our lives . . . Therefore . . . we must always bear this foremost in mind . . . the spirit of our unity will only be what we make of it . . . no more . . . no less.

I did not choose you to be my mate halfheartedly . . . I did so because you have convinced me that you are a . . . just . . . man . . . . A man who will always have my best interests at heart . . . You can rest assured that I will always have your best interests at heart, too.

Mistakes will be made along the way . . . but none intentionally I dare to say.

It is my prayer that my relationship will be a great and holy union and that our joining be a sacred space . . . May the two of us find rest here . . . a haven for our souls.

Remove from us any temptation to judge one another or to direct one another.

May we not be tempted by fantasies and projections . . . as lessons come and challenges grow . . . Let us not be tempted to forsake each other.

May we remain young in this relationship.

May we grow wise in this relationship . . . there are a million and one things that I would like to say to you . . . but for now let me say this . . . I LOVE YOU (full name) with my total being and there is nothing in this world or any other that could make me denounce your honor . . . your truth . . . or my allegiance towards you . . . For I bear witness you are the Light . . . the song . . . and the laughter beneath my wings.

And because your life is more precious to me than even my own . . . I surrender mine to you"

As one can see here, Dawud was always able to perfect his writing to a piece of poetic art.

Forgiveness

I was glad that Dawud always found someone in his environment he could relate to. His family hadn't been much of a support or comfort to him. When his father still lived, they did not have any contact for a long time. Phone calls were a privilege of, maybe, once in three months. His father could not read and write, so the possibility of contact through letters fell away. His mother would write once in a while, but Dawud did not look forward to her letters. She would write to him: "Do you need some money?" In the years I was in South Africa, Dawud had no pocket money to buy paper, stamps or any essentials, so he would answer his mother: "Yes please, send me a little money." But then nothing would come from her. This happened again and again. It was the same as in the past: unfulfilled promises. She knew that he really needed a little help, but she still did not send any money. Even though this was one of the most difficult things to do, Dawud had forgiven his mother for all the terrible abuse. The following is a Christmas letter he wrote to his mother:

"Love will enter immediately into any mind that truly wants it, but it must want it truly. Your task is not to seek for love, but merely to seek and find all the barriers in yourself that you have built against it. *Love waits on welcome, not on time.* If love is sharing, how can you find it except through itself? Offer it and it will come to you, because it is drawn to itself. But offer attack and love will be hidden for it can only live in peace. It is the nature of love to look upon the truth, for there it sees itself. With love in you, you have no need except to extend it."

Both his father and mother died while he was still in prison, but Dawud could not go to any of the funerals. We tried very hard to get him permission from the Department of Criminal Justice to go to his father's funeral, but it was not granted. His father really meant a lot to Dawud, even though he also in the end gave up on his son.

The most faithful to him was and still is his half sister who lives in Michigan. She was the little girl Dawud grew up with in the three years that he lived with his Dad.

Dawud was able to forgive those who harmed him when growing up but he had to battle for a long time to forgive himself.

More Support and Prayers

Besides the support and prayers for his well-being from many of my friends and family, Dawud was well received in the home of a good friend of mine at his first parole to Austin, Texas. These are special people, willing to consider opening their house to a stranger. I knew Johanna for quite some years. We both had worked in the same Waldorf settings. She now lived with her new husband in Austin, Texas. I knew her as a person with deep convictions, stemming from her alliance with the Quaker (Friends) movement as well as with the philosophy behind Waldorf education. She already had an active connection with a person on death row, which she would visit ever so often. Her husband Larry also had a big heart and both of them decided to create this opportunity for Dawud to let him stay in their home upon his release. And so it happened that Dawud was their house guest for half a year. Dawud in turn was able to be an active contributor by doing work in the yard, clean house and paint the kitchen. Because of the *false* parole stipulation that Dawud was *not supposed to be near places where children were,* his hosts could never invite friends with children for a visit, which was really hard on them. This all came to an abrupt halt, when the extended arm of the prison system reached out for Dawud and put him back behind bars.

While stressing once more the importance of having a circle, a community of people surrounding Dawud, I want to mention my family still, especially my family in Switzerland. A photo of Dawud is hanging on the wall in their living room. There is a bit of a language barrier in terms of communication with Dawud, but their interest and good intentions over so many years are phenomenal. They can't wait till Dawud finally can get a passport and visit them!

When their married daughter planned a longer visit to America, she included in her plans to go and see Dawud in person in Texas. This was an important connection for him and for me. In the time that Franziska was in the United States she visited him three times in San Antonio.

Our Friend Michael

I met Michael for the first time in 1979, when I was invited to do Eurythmy workshops at an Anthroposophical conference in Houston, Texas. Michael is a criminal lawyer and has gone out of his way over the years to help Dawud. He was able to represent Dawud two times at meetings with members of the Parole Board. Michael even came to our rescue when the mail room at the prison, where

Dawud then resided, threw away the envelop containing the Joint Income Tax forms, he was supposed to sign. They just threw them in the garbage bin. They only told Dawud that he had received an envelop, but that he was not allowed to have the papers. Dawud never in his life had to bother with tax papers, so it did not mean too much for him. Six weeks later he remembered to tell me about it. I could not risk sending a new set of papers, only to have them tossed out again. This time I sent them to Michael, who put them in an official envelop, showing that it came from Dawud's lawyer. The prison authorities have to give mail from lawyers unopened to the inmates. Dawud could sign the papers now but had to send them back to Michael, who in turn sent them to me. This is again an example of the complications you run into when you are dealing with the Department of Corrections.

The greatest service which Michael has awarded Dawud is to let him stay in his house when he was paroled in September 2007. If Michael would not have made that offer, Dawud would have languished much longer in prison, as no inmate is released unless they have a proper address or the acceptance to a Halfway House, all of which have long waiting lists. I thought that Dawud would join me in California after some time, but could not have foreseen that the Department of Criminal Justice would keep him one and a half years, before taking him off the monitor.

I am glad—no, even stronger—I am extremely thankful that so many friends here in the US and in Europe have been there to support Dawud and me. Dawud is doing his part to live by the endless stipulations he has to deal with when still on parole, and, in addition to that, being electronically monitored twenty-four hours a day. After one and a half year Dawud was finally released from this dehumanizing gadget.

I have already talked about the Special Visitor Erwin, who, in 1980, went to see Dawud in Jackson Prison. I have been in touch with him through all the years, even though he lives in the Netherlands. In his last phone call in March 2009, just before his death ten days later, he expressed his hopes that "Waiting for Dawud" would bring out a clearer picture of this very special human being: Dawud Anglin-Bullis, who is so smart and yet, always gets himself in deep waters, which resulted in his having had to spend a total of thirty-three years in prison.

Dawud has the strong desire to give back to society. Will he be able to do that as long as he is still under the supervision of the Parole Board? In another chapter we will share how he feels he can best contribute to changes of attitude in individual probationers and first time offenders, and also how this could affect the prison system in a positive way.

Chapter Seven

The Effects of Long Term Imprisonment

(written by Truus for the Prison Handbook in 1981)

This writing is based on long term observations and conversations with people who have spent between three and thirty three years in prison. How have these years changed them? Did it have the effect it was intended to have? Or did society breed a new kind of person for better or worse, which it is unable to understand and, therefore, even after the incarceration period is over, is unable to deal with?

It is my belief that, indeed, a new kind of person immerges from the traumatic experience of prison. Let me explain why. The alienation from the "normal" way starts for many people early in life. Before a person in later years rejects society, he or she has been rejected him/herself first. In most of all the case histories of violent offenders, there has been a rejection, abuse, violence or abandonment by the parents and those surrounding the child in the early years.

Out of personal involvement with many three, four and five year olds of low-income inner-city children, I have seen already the hardening of their little souls, unable to cope with too many continuous negative experiences. Their whole beings reflect the No that they have been constantly subjected to. The older the children get, the more hardened they become in their attitude of retaliation: "You have rejected me, I am going to reject you." Without a convincing example of a loving and caring person, this attitude only leads from bad to worse.

One can not expect these youngsters to turn around and choose a better direction out of themselves.

When all good measures do not seem to have any effect, as these bounce off against the armor of seeming indifference and one is unable to reach the good core of the juvenile or adolescent, the young person isolates him/ herself more and more and seeks companionship with those who have gone through similar patterns of rejection, abuse and deprivation. As a group, a gang, they seem to gain a new kind of strength out of 'We against Them'.

This is the path along which the criminal person is bred. He does not get there because his innate being wants to be bad. He is what he is now because of not finding the right cultivation for his soul and his body. He is like a plant that did not get the right soil, was not tended well and withers away. In human terms, withering-away like this means becoming an obstacle for society and for himself.

Karl Menninger*, well-known criminologist, makes this observation in his book Crime and Punishment: "The criminal is a person who for all sorts of reasons is chronically and basically more uncomfortable than most of us. Like us he has internal tensions, but they are heightened by special circumstances, relating to his situation in life. His personal freedom is restricted in a way that is particularly painful to him and his way of regaining some measure of freedom is not ours. The persuasive word, the new proposal, the reasoned argument—for these he has no skill. His constitutional way to deal with his discomfort is by direct action.

There is, before the criminal outbreak, always a sense of helplessness and hopelessness at the bottom of it all. The criminal usually is a person, who had little opportunity to use his creative abilities (in a socially acceptable manner) and planning an illegal act provides an outlet for his potentiality. Many individuals perform criminal acts in order not to "go crazy" or become neurotically inhibited or highly disorganized."

Society may have tried to reach the person on his way downhill; certainly many efforts may have been made, but they do not seem to reach the person any more. It seems that restraining (imprisonment) is turned to as the most obvious solution to deal with those who have turned to criminal activity.

As we now look at the time period people with such backgrounds have been incarcerated, we see new patterns emerge in their lives of soul. They are finally released after years, but, most of the time, they are unable to make it and function in the outside world. After having gone a few times through the revolving door back into prison, they may hit rock bottom. At this point a strong individual will make a decision, to go from bad to worse, or to move in a positive direction. Even if a person embarks on the process of inner rehabilitation, it may take years before a person may completely turn around. Authority has at this point lost any meaning, except when a person starts to recognize the authority of the Master Force of the Universe. It may also be that a person has started to move his attitude towards a positive outlook on life because of a meeting with someone, a clergy man, a caring community person. Often, without the interference of a human being, this is achieved by direct experience of a Higher Power, be it called God, or Allah, or the touch of the Spirit.

The prison society is operating under tremendous pressures, is an intensified society. Our society of the so called "free world" lives in an unbelievable mood of complacency. We believe that we struggle so hard already, that we can't take on anything more, that we are already doing more than our share, but compared to life in prison, we are complacent to the utmost.

The enormous pressures in the prison setting come not only from the prison authorities, from the guards, from the way the system is operating, but also from the ripping violence that exists in the prison. Under these conditions a new kind of person is bred. Only a very strong individual will be able to transcend the extremely negative environment. He will do so, not because of any rehabilitation efforts from the side of the Department of Corrections, but because a healing force has touched him and has made him understand that there is meaning in all his suffering.

All the efforts towards inner rehabilitation still do not take away the damage that is done in the deeper layers of the soul and the finer bodies of the incarcerated person. He is physically confined, restrained and must remain in one spot, but the mind starts wandering disproportionally to overcome the boundaries of the physical obstacles. It will take years to come again to a healthy balance between mind and body after a person has finally been released. In addition to this comes the fact that drugs are easily available in most prisons. Even if a person decides to refrain from using drugs any longer, it is still a big process to overcome the damage done.

When the juvenile has already developed into a "loner", the prison "solution" of putting him away for months, sometimes for a year or more in solitary confinement, has a deep and lasting impact. The extreme opposite from solitary confinement is the situation when all cells are open on one side. The mere fact of being "caged" without any privacy draws the person so deeply into himself that the word loneliness can in no way describe the state of mind anymore, which the person by that time has adopted. Many people with life sentences become as learned in criminal law as the lawyers themselves. This involvement in handling their own cases is an immense strain in the minds, as there is no outlet in relaxed social interaction. Life is a strain from morning till evening. Being constantly subjected to unbearable noise levels and fear for one's own life, as well as all the unpleasantries of poor living conditions effect the inmates, such as broken fixtures, bugs of all kinds, showers too hot or too cold, bad food, the best parts of which regularly disappear on the black market before reaching the inmates. All these inconveniences increase the levels of tension which build up in the individual.

Among the inmates is a wealth of intelligence. It even seems that those who have a greater level of intelligence and a greater sensitivity go more easily off the deep end before they are caught. Once in prison, the intelligent inmate will master the circumstances he is subjected to by using his brains. But there really is no outlet for a person's feelings. Lucky are those who still can express themselves in *art*, which gives them a certain wholesomeness in an insane environment. But those, who have none of this, live with tension levels so high, that we can hardly imagine it.

Somehow, the incarcerated person has learned to cope and stay alive. Finally the date of his release comes, for which he is in no way prepared, because he has not learned responsibility. He has been fed, clothed and housed (warehoused). Now with a hundred dollars in his pocket, he is supposed to make it in a hostile world, a world that constantly will deny employment to anyone with a prison record. So much healing has to take place before anyone with this kind of background can take his or her rightful place in society again.

Shakespeare had some profound words for us in his play "Measure for Measure":

> "Best men are molded out of faults and,
> for the most part, become much better for
> having been a little bad."

Another view we get from the words of Joaquin Miller*:

> "In men whom men condemn as ill,
> I find so much of goodness still.
> In men whom men pronounced divine,
> I find so much of sin and blot.
> I do not dare to draw the line
> Between the two, where God has not."

Archaic Concepts of Crime and Punishment

"The Degree of Civilization in a Society can be Judged by Entering its Prisons"

Dostojewski*

Society has come a long way in how it has been dealing with individuals, who have placed themselves outside the norms and laws of their group or society. In the mid seventeen-hundreds in Britain, people had to endure gruesome tortures before being put to death, which could mean being burned or buried alive. Corporal punishment like the stocks and the pillories, whippings, brandings and amputations, were all executed in plain view of the crowd. Punishment was, in essence, a public spectacle. In many countries of the world today we still find to-day these kinds of ways to punish people. We call them atrocities.

Other modes of punishment included banishment, forced labor in galleys, appropriation of the property of an accused and punitive transportation of large numbers of undesirables. English convicts facilitated the initial colonization of Australia and also settled in Georgia on American soil.

Long term imprisonment only came later, in the eighteenth century, and was a result of changed patterns of thinking during the period of Enlightenment. The new ideologies reflected the rise of the bourgeoisie. The first penitentiary in the United States was opened in 1920.*

By the end of the eighteenth century reformers in England argued that punishment should cease to be revenge and, therefore, had to be executed in isolation behind the walls of a prison. The idea was that law breakers could thus be reformed. We can already see how the idea of crime and punishment changes with the times according to the development of people's soul capacities.

Then came a shift in radical thinking and with that the social perception that the individual had inalienable rights and liberties. This was as much a result of the French Revolution as it was from the American Revolution. Now, in the twenty-first century we are still holding on to the concepts which were formed during the eighteenth and nineteenth centuries. Sadly enough, these rights were then not extended to women, workers, blacks and Indians. *

Another means of punishment, mostly practiced under communism, was <u>shaming.</u> This was a way of forcing "deviants" to come back into the fold of accepted group norms.

Punishing with "Doing Time"

Strangely enough the Age of Reason and the rise of science brought about the abstract quantifications of punishment by removing the individual from society and <u>handing out "time"</u> to be served in penitentiaries. The idea was that inmates could be reformed and do penance by placing them in individual cells in complete isolation. Charles Dickens wrote already in 1842, after his visit to the Eastern Penitentiary, that "the system here is rigid, strict and hopeless solitary confinement. I believe it is, in its effects, to be cruel and wrong. I believe that very few men are capable of estimating the immense amount of torture and agony that this dreadful punishment, prolonged for years, inflicts upon the sufferers. There is a depth of terrible endurance in it which none but the sufferers themselves can fathom, and which no man has a right to inflict upon his fellow-creatures. I hold this slow and daily tampering with the mysteries of the brain to be immeasurable worse than any torture of the body . . . because its wounds are not upon the surface, and it extorts few cries that human ears can hear; therefore, I the more strongly denounce it as a secret punishment which slumbering humanity is not roused to stay."

In 1870 the American Correctional Association laid down twenty-two Principles, of which four follow here:

- Reformation, not vindictive suffering should be the purpose of the penal treatment of prisoners
- The prisoner should be made to realize that his destiny is at his own hands.
- Prison discipline should be such as to gain the will of the prisoner and conserve his self-respect.
- The aim of the prison should be to make industrious free men rather than orderly and obedient prisoners.

How is it possible that we lost so much of our true humanity? Are we regressing in our culture instead of progressing? Will it be possible that we find a way back to the ethical principles we were capable of in the past?

Another model added to the solitary cells was the prison labor, performed by groups, but done in absolute silence. The idea still was <u>Rehabilitation</u>. But what was the purpose of the rehabilitation? The working class needed to be constituted as an army of self-disciplined individuals, capable of performing the requisite industrial labor for the developing capitalist system.*

<u>Solitary Confinement</u>

To-day solitary confinement is used broadly and is considered by the inmates the worst of punishment. Dawud spent fourteen months in solitary confinement. This kind of treatment can break a person in a short time or make him ever stronger in defiance. The Criminal Justice System of to-day has not just added more and more prisons, it has added increased numbers of Supermax prisons, where inmates often are kept for years in total isolation. They live in windowless cells, four by eight feet, for twenty-three hours a day. In their exercise time they are allowed into a small cage. Usually they are solitary and they are given no program. <u>By now all references to individual rehabilitation have disappeared.</u>

<u>The Unbridled Expansion of the Prison System</u>

The prison system has grown tenfold in the last thirty years. Two million people are behind bars on any given day. The United States has more people imprisoned than any other country in the world—half a million more than in Communist China—and consists of the largest prison expansion the world has ever known. One in four African-American men, one in six Hispanic men and one in ten white men will go to prison in their life times!* "What makes us Americans so hateful and uncaring that we house 25% of the world's inmates? Why is a black male in California more likely to go to a state prison than to a state college? When during an economic crunch funds for education, health—and social services are cut, we are still spending $200 billion annually on law enforcement. And corrections employs more Americans than the combined work forces of General Motors, Ford and Wal-Mart together." (From "America Incarcerated. Crime and Punishment and the Question of Race", Boston Review, November/December 2007) Do we need to boost employment at the horrific human cost of imprisoning ever more people?

I want to add some of the latest facts about the American prisons, as published in Newsweek of June 2009*. Now that so much emphasis is on Guantanamo, the focus comes back to the overall prison situation here. "The United States with 5 percent of the world's population, houses nearly 25 percent of the world's prisoners."

As Webb has explained it, "We're either the most evil people on earth, or we're doing something wrong". "We incarcerate 756 inmates per 100,000 residents—nearly five times the world average. Approximately one in every thirty-one adults in the United States is in prison, in jail or in supervised release."

The Supermax Prisons

With video cameras and remote-controlled electronic doors modern prisons, and especially the supermaxes, rely on state-of-the-art technology for monitoring and controlling prisoner conduct and movement.

Let us hear what Jonathan T. Hallinan* writes as the final conclusion of his book Going up the River: "What I found was the perfectly evolved American prison. It was both lavishly expensive and needlessly remote, built not because it was needed, but because it was wanted: by politicians, who thought it would bring them votes, wanted by voters, who hoped it would bring jobs, and by the corrections establishment that no longer believed in corrections.

A win-win for everybody, except for the inmates."

What, in human terms, is the price we pay? Prisons are no longer places to reform or rehabilitate, prisons are now viewed as a source of economic development.

The Prison Industrial Complex

"For private business, prison labor is like a pot of gold. No strikes. No union organizing. No health benefits, unemployment insurance or workers' compensation to pay. No language barriers as in foreign countries. New leviathan prisons are being built on thousands of eerie

acres, but they are basically factories inside the walls. Prisoners do data entry for Chevron, make telephone reservations for TWA, raise hogs and shovel manure. They make circuit boards, limousines, waterbeds, and lingerie for Victoria's Secret, all at a fraction of what it would cost in the free world."
(Linda Evans and Eve Goldberg, "The Prison Industrial Complex and the Global Economy" Prison Activist Resource Center 1997 Berkeley, California)

Relatively little is known of what happens behind the walls. Inmates would have a lot to say, but only a few, who have had an education before being incarcerated or the few who were able to do this through their own tenacious efforts, are able to write about the system and their experiences. Fortunately we have a book written by inmate Jens Soering* "An Expensive Way to Make Bad People Worse". The book exposes the untenable situation of the whole Criminal Justice System in an expert way. In its foreword by a former prison warden, we find a sad appraisal of the criminal justice to-day, as it has deteriorated over the years

The Criminal Justice System To-day

This is how a retired Director of the Alaska Department of Corrections views the current situation: "When I began my first job in the field of corrections more than fifty years go, I hardly anticipated that as the time came for me to more or less fold my tent, I would be feeling a heavy sense of disillusionment. In choosing a career I had been prompted by a certain measure of idealism, as had many of my colleagues of that era. How could any of us have known that by the mid-1970s the field of endeavor we had chosen would be in the process of marginalizing all notions of imagination, hope and compassion, or that due to the politics of that time the very concept of rehabilitation would be viewed as discredited? The most cynical among us would not have predicted that the imprisonment function of the criminal justice system in America would have *spiraled down into hardly more than human warehousing.* The idea of more than two million people in American jails and penitentiaries would have been beyond the imagination of any of us."*

How does the Criminal Justice Department manage to incarcerate not only more and more people, but also to keep people longer and longer in prison:

- By handling drug addiction not with treatment but with incarceration
- By judges handing out longer and longer sentences (one out of every eleven inmates is now a "lifer")
- By doing away with "good time" earned in prison
- By not releasing very old and sick inmates
- By releasing fewer and fewer inmates altogether
- Through the Three Strikes Law

Since 1995, all fifty states in America have spent more on prisons than on colleges, a trend that has accelerated since then. Prison guards are paid higher salaries than school teachers.

How is it possible that tax payers, the general population, accepts the fact that prisons have become a financial burden on the budgets of the states without delivering the positive results in the form of people being rehabilitated? People don't accept it if the garage where they bring their cars for repairs, doesn't fix them properly.

Jens Soering, who is serving a double life sentence for murder, writes in the conclusion at the end of his book:

"This country's current addiction to jails and prisons is a betrayal of America's core value: LIBERTY. Once this was "the land of the free", but no longer. And that betrayal of the heart of the American dream has moral consequences. Every single US citizen who pays taxes directly supports the correctional culture and thus is paying for the slow destruction of his or her own identity as an American."

It is my hope that the economic crisis will help people to see that the incarceration craze is untenable. *"The average prisoner in Pennsylvania costs the tax payer $33,615 for a year in prison. For about $25,000 he could get a college education." California, a state with a huge budget deficit, spent $8.8 billion on Corrections in 2007 and its prison guards $10,000 more per year than its teachers. The combined spending in the country for law enforcement and corrections is about $200 billion.

Dealing with the System from a Personal Point of View

Beyond statistics, how did I personally, in my own life, feel the impact of this colossal monster, called the Criminal Justice System? I, after all, have had to deal with it for thirty years.

The original title of this book was "Waiting for Dawud" which expresses strongly the element of WAITING. It meant that I went together with him each time through endless waiting for the next parole interview, which is supposed to happen once a year. Each time, hopes for release would be high only to be dashed year after year. This was not because Dawud had any disciplinary tickets or any unacceptable behavior held against him. Does one get an explanation why there is time and again another set-off? Dawud never got any reasons for the set-offs, only short letters stating the fact that he would not be released for another year. Another year!

How does a prisoner deal with these constant deep disappointments? How is it for the family? How was it for me, his wife, to be ready to receive my husband home year after year, but then to hear again that it is not happening? When I got the bad news from him, my thoughts would always go first to Dawud and how much worse it was for him. I tried to cheer him up the best way I could, but he still had to creep out of the hole of desperation by himself.

Should one try to see the working of the System as a necessary evil because of the overwhelming amount of prisoners it has to deal with? One can't, as one is too much aware of the fact that the System was created to subdue the unruly masses, that the System came to its ridiculous expansion as politicians played more and more on the fear of the people and got their cooperation (meaning their votes) by promising that life would finally be made safe and secure for the law-abiding people.

Those incarcerated, called inmates, are numbers. Dawud should write about that himself. Over the years I got engaged in endless letter writing to authorities in the System, not because I thought it would bring us something, but to help Dawud to feel that he was not just a pawn in the chess game. The issues dealt with in the letters were, so to say, whisked off the table of the receiving party as non-existent. Lawyers may still have some impact, but as we found out, also only a very small amount. We were very fortunate to have a best friend who is a lawyer, who engaged himself pro bono in behalf of us many times.

He went with me several times to meet with a member of the Parole Board in Huntsville, Texas. The strategy from the side of the Parole Board was to let us speak, but never come up themselves with any concrete answers. All the efforts led to nowhere.

Dawud had real issues that needed to be dealt with. The fact that he got a stipulation upon his release to Austin of having "Restrictions involving minors" was like being accused of pedophilia. There was in his whole history no indication in that direction, so this needed urgent rectification. I have described this in greater detail in Chapter Five under the heading 'Release and Paroled to Austin, Texas'. It took the Department of Criminal Justice a *full four years* until Dawud finally received a rectification from this "mistake". This happened only after we paid a lawyer big money to put pressure on the situation. This shows that the Criminal Justice System can make serious mistakes, which can cost a prisoner many more years to "serve".

The Criminal Justice System is also capable of black-mailing. It is obvious that I can't go into details about the actuality of these happenings. Higher-ups in the Department have on the screen before them all the information about each prisoner. They can use it illegally when a parolee has made even the smallest infraction on the rules, which could put that person back into prison. Unless one pays sizable amounts of money, that is exactly what will happen.

When finally a person is paroled, life does not become any easier, especially not when a person like Dawud is attached to an electronic monitor. His official parole reaches up to the year 2013. Making the slightest mistake, is already a reason to revoke the parole and to be returned to prison. This may be the inability to pay for the classes you have to take. In Dawud's case, he has to attend three classes a week. There is no excuse whatsoever to be absent, even if he is very sick and has a high fever. Shortly after being paroled, Dawud was told that they would not process any paper work requesting his transfer to California, unless he paid up for college classes he took while still in prison. That was an amount of $1200. I was very lucky to find a relative of mine willing to help him out by paying this amount. The inability to pay the fees for all the classes can be a reason to be returned to prison. The fees are $40 and $20 per class per week; $75 for a conversation with the treatment provider, $250 for a lie detector's test, which Dawud already had to take three times since his release, which means a cost of $750 in addition to all the other costs which are a Workbook for $20, a Screening Test for $275 and an Intake Fee of $30. This adds up for only 20 weeks to an amount of $1895.

Dawud was very lucky that he found work—low paying as is, but it is a job. Not finding a job as well as the inability to pay for the treatment fees can all be reasons to be returned to prison. Dawud found this job himself but was given several reasons by the parole officer why he could not take this job because there was a bar next door or there was a McDonalds across the street. These objections had no legal basis, which Dawud had to point out to the Parole Supervisor. Only his perseverance and determination got him this job. Even though he works six days a week and has a room for free at the house of our lawyer friend, he can hardly exist on his earnings because he has to pay so much all the time to the TDCJ.

To begin with, Dawud had to take the Sex Offender classes for half a year in Austin. After the Technical Parole Violation he had to take these same classes in prison for another half year. This was the reason they kept him years beyond his release date. In addition, he was told that he had to take these same Sex Offender classes once again when on parole in San Antonio, which by now has been again one and a half years. This adds up to two and half years of having to take the Same Sex Offender classes!

<u>One has to bear in mind that the Sexual Assault, involving his second wife from whom he already was divorced, was a one-time situation which happened</u> **twenty-one years ago**!

The Electronic Monitor

The prison system uses of all the modern high tech possibilities, but especially for certain ex-offenders when on parole by having them wear an electronic monitor. With that system they can check up on the wearer of the monitor twenty-four hours, day and night. Not to make a mistake is nerve racking. Dawud had this gadget attached to him for half a year when he was paroled in Austin; he has been wearing this ankle bracelet again since September 2007. Finally, after 20 months, in April of 2009, he finally was given the freedom to move about without this gadget. Are parolees given any indication when they might be taken of the monitor? The answers can be, "When you have paid up your fees for the classes", or, "When you have taken the lie detector's test". After he had done all that, he, the parolee, asks again: "When will I get off the monitor?" This brings more evasive answers. Dawud had to ask around among the other parolees, waiting in the parole office, to find out more. Some had been on the monitor for already more than two years. For the Parole Board to decide on this can take several months. So the "Love in Action" that had to be actualized, was not just for the years he spent in prison. It continued long after he had been paroled

Once one is caught in the system, it doesn't let go. The philosophy, obviously, is "Once bad, always bad". There is no way to determine if a prisoner or a parolee has really changed.

This is for me the most important reason to write this book, to show that even a career criminal can make a total turn around. Imagine the wealth of wisdom a person can bring to society who has gone through all this horror, induced first by himself, then by the system. Dawud has an urge to give back to society. His plans in this direction are to be found under the heading "Change Instead of Chains".

Chapter Eight

In the Belly of the Beast

Over the years, I have often asked Dawud what life in prison is like. When I visited him—which was not so often because of the big distances between us—he wasn't interested to speak about what it was like inside, because the few hours we had, either in the visiting room or on the phone behind a separation window, would be so precious that he did not want to spoil our time together. It could happen, though, that he would be unable to make a smooth transition from the "belly of the beast" to the visiting room, specifically to me, and that, for a while, he was unable to let go of his whole pent-up energy and survival mentality. At one time it took me a full visit of four hours to slowly ease him back into gentler reality. Luckily we had the next day still with another four hours to really enjoy each other as human beings on the same plane. Once in a while he would share his deep frustrations in his letters, which gave me then a much fuller picture of what it might like inside. I'll let Dawud speak for himself.

"I'm not even going to try anything serious. My mind is in too much of a pensive whirl-wind. Fortunately, I was able to trade my dinner for two sheets of writing paper, but since I have no stamps or envelopes, I don't know when I will be able to mail this. I know that it is actually impossible for any civilian, even you, to fathom what it is truly like to be in a gulag, and I could never in a million years explain it clearly enough where you would be able to grasp the horrors it contains, but the major difference between my state of existence and yours is, that everything in here is ferociously intensified, just about everyone has a hair trigger attitude and you can quickly loose your life over something as trivial as a pack of cigarettes, a look in the wrong direction, or a word spoken at the wrong time—to the wrong person. Simply stated, it is a war zone, the worst imaginable, because in this war, your adversary is not wearing a different uniform and he's not in one trench and you're in another, you have to interact, i.e., eat, sleep and shower with him daily." Dawud told me that in certain prisons he had to use 70% of his awareness to plainly stay alive.

"This continuous engagement (because it's mostly psychological) can literally smash your psyche to a withering pulp. But, because of the amount of years I've served and had to deal with zombie-like people, who can't think for themselves, I'm able to handle or step around most conflicts and negative situations. However, there is always that one unexpected event lurking in the shadows, waiting to leap out and devour you. Such is the case with my present predicament. I could have been eaten alive, swallowed whole, but I managed to escape the clutches of the dragon, thanks mostly to the grace of my guardian angel and my adherence to the strict code of silence which exist in all gulags. In here, nothing gets the life snuffed out of you quicker than loose lips . . ."

"Allow me to tell you something about that old cliché of 'reaching down and pulling yourself up by your own boot straps'. Fundamentally, I endorse both the pertinence and validity of its incentiveness, but when your whole constitution has been stressed to the max—more time than you want to remember and you've suffered more than most people could ever comprehend, let alone endure themselves, and then some air-head (usually it's a stranger) comes mirthfully along and says, "quit your whining and sniveling and pull your sorry ass up by your boot straps", even though they might mean well, you would like to scream into their little narrow mind, "What the hell do you think I have been doing my whole life?" Still, there's always that dreaded fear of one day reaching down and not finding any straps left to grab a hold of. If this nightmare were ever to come true, I'd sever all ties with you and this world, as my heart could not contain the agony of you knowing what I had become. So you must always bear this reality in mind, as long as I'm in prison, I'm only one small step from having the beast drag me down into his lair . . . ."

"I had a very soul expanding experience this morning, one which I'm sure St. Michael sent, as he knew I desperately needed it to assure me that my heart still has life in it. While I was eating breakfast I got to thinking about all those children who at this very moment in Africa are dying from starvation. Suddenly, I couldn't eat another single bite. Then I got angry, and my rage had nitroglycerin in it because I started thinking about who the real hard-core criminals are in this world. They're certainly not the majority of the ones in prison. We're just little guppies compared to the bureaucratic sharks and political werewolves who, on a global scale practice their parasiticpolitics on the masses. My heart is howling because everybody on this planet is directly or indirectly responsible for what's happening to these starving children".

Dealing with Depression

The other side of the emotional spectrum can easily get prisoners into states of depression, which is likely to occur after having been turned down again by the Parole Board. "I've been in a severe funk, which I can't, for the life in me, shake off. I've also been completely void of any creativity; even reading (which has always been one of my greatest loves and greatest escapes too) now bores me to smithereens! When I'm not working, all I want to do is sleep, pout, watch all the mindless nonsense on T.V. and endlessly bitch about all the injustices in my life, just like all the other ninety-eight percent of the inmate population.

Hopefully I'll soon be able to crawl out from under this cursed yoke of depression, as its wretchedness is ever so slowly starting to strangle what little sensibility I have left. Besides, I've got a lot of unfinished projects on the drawing board, which are in dire need of my attention. I am terribly disappointed in myself to have to admit this, Truus. There's a painting Van Gogh did in 1890, when he was at the asylum at Saint Remy, which, besides, is his self-portrait, my absolute favorite. I love this painting with a forthright passion. Try and get a look at it, particularly a close-up of his eyes. Because the same tormented expression, that's emanating from them, is identical to the expression that's now emanating from mine."

Yet, the poet in Dawud still can say, "I've

been adrift in this transient sea with a cold hollow wind blowing through the marrow of my bones for far longer than the nightingale has ever waited the morning."

While trying to maintain a sense of self, a prisoner always has to act subservient. As the years in prison for Dawud accumulated, he was on the one hand very aware not to say anything to a guard and get himself in difficulties, but in the case of degrading treatment, he would show the guard the words he had written at the back of his identity card, which said, "If I react to a fool, what would make that out of me? A fool." Often guards try to provoke inmates, so they can write them up for a disciplinary ticket. There were times, though, that he felt he could not take the whole dehumanizing prison environment any longer. He once wrote to me, "I used to think that I couldn't be broken, but I'm not so sure of that now. I am weary, Truus, and I think you are too. Considering what we have been through, we have every cause to be."

The Effect of Set-Offs

The set-offs (denial of parole) happened so many times during the many years that Dawud was in prison. This is one of Dawud's reactions at one such occasion: "After I received the Parole Board's mind-boggling notification, I was so incredibly angry and suffered such deep humiliation that I regressed into a sort of semi-catatonic state and did not leave my cell for almost ten days. I couldn't eat, I couldn't sleep, I couldn't do anything but sit in my cell and stare vacant-eyed at the wall like some type of pathetic zombie. I can hardly describe the state of mind I was in except to say, it was a combination of fear, intense sadness and extreme confusion at life' injustices".

"It's a bloody nightmare waiting to receive notice from the Board. I've been trying to keep what little sense I've got left to pre-occupy myself with various activities, but the more I try not to think about what's going to happen, the more I dwell on the matter. It's like a leaking faucet. You try to ignore the drip, drip, drip, but it just keeps getting louder and louder. Now I know why they invented the Chinese water torture."

One has to keep in mind that minor infractions can lead to the denial of parole. Letters, going out and coming in, are always censored. Dawud had written to his former wife that "he would not and could not allow her to stand in the way of letting him see his daughter". This was the reason for the set-off. According to the Parole Board's reasoning it was a threatening letter.

One can imagine what it takes to pull oneself again out of the hole of being rejected at yet another set-back. At one time Dawud wrote: "I had narrow-mindedly psyched myself into believing that after three set-offs and serving over seven years, they were actually going to release me this time. What a bloody fool I was! The only option I have is to request a special review and file a brief in Federal

Court for unlawful and/or excessive incarceration, but I'll need your assistance because it's going to cost me fifty dollars to pay a paralegal."

Dawud could always vent his frustrations with me. To have someone to write to is more than most inmates have. The longer Dawud was imprisoned, the more difficult it got, this endless waiting game. You can't ask any of the authorities to get any answers. Dawud mostly had to go by what he might find out through the grapevine, how other inmates with similar situations to his were treated. Especially the last spell between 2002 and 2007 was the hardest time Dawud had ever done. The more unreasonable this meting out of time seemed to be, the harder it was to "do time". There is one axiom prisoners try to live by: "Never count days, weeks or months". Imagine how much self-discipline it takes to do that. In one of the letters from this time he says that "one of the things I have learned from you and my studies in Anthroposophy, is to view matters/issues from a collective overview."

After a very long wait Dawud was once more transferred in 2004 to yet another prison in Texas. When he got there, the prison was at first on lock-down. This is supposed to be for contraband (weapons and drugs) searches. That happens periodically in every prison wherever Dawud has been. It means that for at least five days no one is leaving his cell and the men are given only brown bags, containing peanut butter and jelly sandwiches. Usually every few days inmates can purchase necessities like paper and stamps from a commissary cart, but not during these days. After the lock-down was over, Dawud finally could get paper and tell me: "Right now I am alone in my cell because my cellie has gone to church. This is the first time that I've been entirely alone in twenty months. It's a queer feeling that no one is watching me 24-7. It's quiet too. The cell block I am in is populated by men who are almost all over forty. I'm going to go to recreation tomorrow. I've heard that they've got real grass that you can walk around on. A special treat as I haven't walked on mother earth in twenty months."

Besides lock-downs I have to mention that cell blocks are regularly gassed. According to Dawud this is so bad. One can not stop breathing, so one gets the full load of chemicals ingested. "Your eyes are watering and for days you are nauseous and have to cough." There is no hiding place when you are locked up.

How was Dawud able to keep up with his health under these unhealthy circumstances? I would say by pure will power. As he said: "Nothing will get me down". In one prison Dawud never went outside for months on end because the only hour set aside for outdoor recreation was before sundown or after sunset. Yet, Dawud seldom was physically sick. As he tells me, he was an exception to the rule. He would exercise a lot in his cell, do push-ups, even jog on the spot for hours. Sometimes I asked Dawud the question "Who Are You?" I myself lived all those years and am still living with the question: Who is this person I got so close to for so long, who nevertheless, since 1979, was always so far away.

Finally paroled

In September 2007, Dawud finally got paroled, this time to San Antonio, Texas. I was going to be there to receive him, so we happened to arrive both at the same time at the house of our mutual friend Michael, Dawud's parole address. It was difficult for me to fathom in what state of mind my husband might be. Yes, there was the joy of finally being out of the belly of the beast. But because he had to deal from day one with the fact of being attached to an ankle bracelet, to the electronic monitoring system, he really wasn't free. Dawud was very anxious not to make any mistake. It wasn't always clear what the exact boundaries of the monitoring system were. Must he stay in the house, or could he go onto the backyard where the washer and drier were installed? Any mistake could be fatal, as going back to prison now would be like a life sentence. That's why my three weeks with him had some lovely moments but also a few blow-ups, as he could not relax and was basically on edge all the time.

We did not know how the parole officer would deal with the idea of a transfer of Dawud to me in California, I thought that he might come after maybe one month. Not so. After one and a half years Dawud still was in San Antonio. I elaborated earlier what it means to be on the electronic monitor. When he was finally released from this torturous instrument, I thought it would make a tremendous difference to him to have this element of freedom. Because his imprisonment was basically continued by having to live up to an exact hourly schedule and he could only work at the one restaurant or stay on Sundays locked up in Michael's house, he did not get to know any other people. One can say that he had to invent his life once more from the bottom up.

Chapter Nine

<u>Ethical Considerations</u>

> "The degree of civilization of a country can be
> judged by entering its prisons"
> (Feodor Mikhailovich Dostojewski)

<u>The Need to Rethink Corrections</u>

The moment the politicians stop preying on people's fears, while promising absolute safety and security from crime and criminals, we may be able to start thinking clearly again. We will realize that America has lost its way by creating a monstrous prison system, which on the one hand, seems an excellent way for the use of cheap labor, yet plays itself out on the lives of the millions of people, locked up and warehoused in concrete bunkers, who basically have been stripped of their citizenship. Let us look once more at Dostojewski's statement: "The degree of civilization can be judged by entering its prisons." In olden times punishment was executed in the market square. Then we created the walled-in prisons. It is a closed world where anything can happen and we will only hear about it when a major riot has occurred. The visitor will enter the prison compound through the outer gate over a walkway, festooned with flowers on both sides. The idea is to make a good impression. This has been the same in each prison I have visited. The visitors' room is still a somewhat civilized place. The prisoners are at their best when they have a visit. But seldom do we have the opportunity to see what is going on inside the prison. This book is able to give the double perspective, the one from the outsider and the one from the inmate.

The Human Kindness Foundation

Bo and Sita Lozoff of The Human Kindness Foundation* have reached thousands of prisoners through their visits in more than a thousand prisons and through their mailing list. Their take on the situation in the USA is well expressed in an article, called <u>Can We Do Better Than Our Present Prison System</u>. "Prisoners currently sleep on floors, in tents, in converted broom closets and gymnasiums, or in double or triple bunk beds in cells that were designated for one inmate. For the most part, prisons are barbaric, terrifying places. Crime victims derive no benefit from this misery. The system offers convicts no opportunities to learn compassion or to take responsibility for what they have done, nor to make restitution or to offer atonement to their victims in practical ways.

Approximately 240,000 brutal rapes occur in our prison system each year. Most of the victims are young, *non-violent* male inmates, many of them teen-agers first-offenders. Unfortunately, many of those non-violent offenders will no longer be non-violent by the time they leave prison. **Prisons are not scaring offenders away from crime; they are incapacitating them so they are**

hardly fit for anything else. In other words, the criminal justice system for which we're paying such a high price, simply isn't working. How do we start fixing what is broken? Only about 10% of the prison population sets the brutal tone for most institutions, and they are able to do that because the administration gives no support to the vast majority of inmates who just want to do their time, improve themselves in some way, and get out alive.

For decades our prison system has been run according to the tenets of "retributive justice", a model based on exile and hatred. "Restorative justice", instead, holds that, when a crime occurs, there's an injury to the community and that injury needs to be healed".

<u>Compassion versus Rage</u>

"There are simple universal laws of human life that cannot be violated without paying a high price. Every great spiritual, philosophic and religious tradition has emphasized compassion, reconciliation, forgiveness and responsibility. These are not suggestions, they are instructions. If we follow them we will thrive, if not we will suffer. The socially-sanctioned hatred and rage that we express towards criminals in modern times violates these timeless instructions. Our children inherit these destructive attitudes. We must realize that we are all part of the problem. If you vote, if you pay taxes, if you are afraid to walk alone at night, you are already involved. And so we have a choice to be solely in negative, destructive ways, such as home security systems, car alarms, personal weapons, etc. or in constructive ways. We all must make real changes—not just political ones, but in our personal attitudes and lifestyles. America will not thrive, nor will we and our children be happy, by becoming a nation behind bars".

We need to know, what is done in our name and with our tax dollars. In a democracy, it is the voice of everybody that counts and must be heard. Ted Conover*, a journalist who masqueraded three years as a prison guard in the Sing Sing prison, gives us a first hand account of life behind the walls. His book "Newjack" (newjack is the name for a rookie guard) gives us insights into the harsh prison culture. Through Conover's eyes we can begin to see how our burgeoning prison system brutalizes everyone connected with it. Soon after the book was published it was declared contraband. New York State officers were not allowed to bring it into the prison, and inmates who had already received copies in the mail, had their books confiscated. Later, in lectures about the book Conover said that one of the reasons he wrote the book was because "the state has unfairly reserved the right to keep prison operations away from public scrutiny". Even though "Newjack" had been written from a guard's perspective, it surely helps to bring a little more transparency into the hidden world behind those big walls and barbed wire.

Conover sees two ways which could help bring about a change in the whole correctional system: 1. States need to repeal mandatory sentencing for drug offenses.

2. Nothing lowers recidivism rates better than education.

We are talking here about *Prevention*. Prisons should be for violent criminals, not mainly for poor men from rough neighborhoods. "Prisons" in his words, "are the unhappy symptom of our violent and grossly unequal society".

Albert Schweitzer's* words show us that his expectations go beyond the judgment of crime and remind us that, "A new Renaissance has to come about in which mankind realizes that the ethical is the highest truth and the most effective one".

As we saw in Chapter Eight from the history of crime and punishment through the ages: we got stuck in patterns of thought which *disregarded the dignity of the prisoner.* We lure businessmen into making profits, and, as a result of the massive incarceration, created an industry built on cheap labor.

We are not only taking away the dignity from the prisoner, we degrade ourselves by making economic gains the highest priority. We need to rethink the idea of punishment and start to think of a justice system that is based on <u>reparation and reconciliation.</u>

"If we take people for what they *are*, we only can make them worse. When we treat them, as if they already are what they *should be*, we help them on their way where they want to be." (Goethe)

<u>Justice</u>

True justice has first to do with the healing of the wounds of society. We hear from Helen Prejean* that "taking on the struggles of the poor (and marginalized people) means invariably, challenging the wealthy and those who serve their interest." The American Friends have, for a long time, been at the forefront of promoting justice, but they too know that as long as equal justice is correlated with equality of status, influence and economic power, the construction of a just system of criminal justice in an unjust society is a contradiction in terms.

This book has not in the first place been written for politicians. They mostly count on our fearful attitude towards crime. As long as we don't muster up to our own courage, they will be in charge. Was I fearful of going into the prison to do Eurythmy with eight male prisoners? No, I had in mind to give them something substantial for their lives. We may learn from the Dog Whisperer that, in relation to lower instincts, it all depends on our attitude in how we meet them. A comparison can be made with people. Fear attracts negative reactions.

I had to experience this again and again in my situation with Dawud. As soon as the landlord in California, from whom I rented the house, heard via neighbors a rumor that Dawud might come home, I was told to move out on short notice. If the landlord only had known that it would take took seven years until Dawud was finally released and then only to Texas, he might have acted differently, but he did not inquire directly with me what the situation was. It was painful for me that the landlord, a person, whom I knew, really believes in the inner striving of the human being to become a better person, had separated his deepest beliefs from what the neighborhood would think of him by allowing an ex-con to live in his house. Fear replaces clear thinking. The heart is silenced.

How Secure is Security?

Has life become safer and more secure because of the politicians' decisions to allow more and more prisons to be built? We may want to listen to some people who overcame enormous obstacles in their lives like Helen Keller*: "Security is mostly a superstition. It does not exist in nature, nor do the children of men as a whole experience it. Avoiding danger is no safer in the long run than outright exposure. Life is either a daring adventure or nothing at all!"

Our courage comes from the trust that whatever happens in life has deep meaning. Rudolf Steiner summons us to overcome fear.

"We must eradicate from the soul all fear and terror of
what comes towards man from the future.
We must acquire serenity in all feelings and sensations
about the future."

I seems to me that we are globally in an enormous learning curve with the economic downturn, the many natural disasters, the changing world, the changing climate, and all other seeming adversity.

The following poem can give us much food for thought:

Because the real truth is not in the truth,
But in the errors, which have been overcome.
And the true reality is not in the reality,
But in the illusion which has been overcome.
And the true purity is not in the original purity,
But in the cleansed impurity.
And the true good is not the original good,
But evil which has been overcome.
This holds true for the whole universe, including the gods.
As on the path, on which evil has been overcome,
Something can develop, which was not
Originally enclosed in the good.
By the fact that God chose to create the adversary forces
He has forced Himself to reveal
His deepest being, even in another way
Than he could have done without them

Friedrich Benesch*

Future Options

The following story as related by Joe Vitale*may seem far fetched, but it can give us an indication of what some of us are already capable now and of what many more can be in the future.

"Two years ago, I heard about a therapist in Hawaii who cured a complete ward of criminally insane patients—without ever seeing any of them. The psychologist would study an inmate's chart and then look within himself to see how he had created that persons illness. As he improved himself, the patient improved."

When I (Joe Vitale) first heard this story, I thought it was an urban legend. How could anyone heal anyone else by healing himself? How could even the best self-improvement master cure the criminally insane? It didn't make any sense. It wasn't logical, so I dismissed the story. However, I heard it again a year later. I heard that the therapist had used a Hawaiian healing process called Ho'oponopono. I had never heard of it, yet I couldn't let it leave my mind. If the story was at all true, I had to know more. I had always understood "total responsibility" to mean that I am responsible for what I think and do. Beyond that, it's out of my hands. I think that most people think of total responsibility that way. We're responsible for what we do, not what anyone else does—but that's wrong.

The Hawaiian therapist who healed those mentally ill people would teach me an advanced new perspective about total responsibility. His name is Dr. Ihaleakala Hew Len. I asked him to tell me the complete story of his work as a therapist. He explained that he worked at Hawaii State Hospital for years. That ward where they kept the criminally insane was dangerous. Psychologists quit on a monthly basis. The staff called in sick a lot or simply quit. People would walk through the ward with their backs against the wall, afraid of being attacked by patients. It was not a pleasant place to live, work or visit.

Dr. Len told me that he never saw patients. He agreed to have an office and to review the files. While he looked at those files, he would work on himself. As he worked on himself, the patients began to heal.

According to Dr. Len, "After a few months, patients that had to be shackled were being allowed to walk freely. Others who had to be heavily medicated were getting off their medications. And those who had no chance of ever being released were being freed. The staff began to enjoy coming to work. Absenteeism and turnover disappeared. We ended up with more staff than we needed because patients were being released. To-day the ward is closed."

This is, says Joe Vitale, where I had to ask the million dollar question: "What were you doing within yourself that caused those people to change?"

And Dr. Len: "I was simply healing the part in me that created them."

So far, this was Joe Vitale's story.

Putting this story next to the whole development of the mega prison boom in this country, we can see that we have a long way to go. It is up to each one of us to rethink how we want to look at crime and criminality.

How can Society Benefit from Dawud's Unique Experience?

Dawud's story shows the origins of his inner imbalance, how he despised the world for what it had done to him, but how he came around and found a new inner certainty that he would never ever hurt anybody anymore.

Instead of only struggling to survive with an ordinary job, as is happening right now, Dawud should be given the opportunity to be invited by high school principals to speak to young people. This had already happened when he still was in prison. Because he had made such an impression on the juveniles who, being on probation, were given the experience of 'A Day in Prison', the principal of the high school which they attended, asked the Warden, if he would allow Dawud to come to his school to address all the students. This request was honored and the Deputy Warden took it upon himself to accompany Dawud on this unusual trip. The Deputy Warden did not want Dawud to go in shackles (hand and feet), but Dawud requested it, as it would make a much deeper impression on the students. And so it happened.

Dawud already has a B.A. in Psychology, classes he took in the prison. It has been suggested by many that he should now get a Masters Degree in Criminology as a person with a degree mostly has greater credibility than a 'mere ex-con'. As a motivational speaker he could have a tremendous impact on the lives of scores of young people, since his every word will be filled with life experience.

Project Last Chance

Already in 1997 Dawud presented a proposal for Project Last Chance to the warden of the Ramsey One Unit in Rosharon, Texas. The idea and inspiration for Project Last Chance was born out of a thank you letter that he received from a nineteen-year-old probationer who said, "The talk we had in the prison changed my life". In Dawud's words: "Initially he had been recommended by the Brazoria County Probation Department to experience the stark realities of a day spent in a Texas prison in a program entitled: "PRISON FOR A DAY". At the conclusion of said day, participants would be brought into a conference room and addressed by veteran correctional officers and a group of well-seasoned inmates of which I'm one. They explained in graphic terms and very matter-of-fact language what they can expect to encounter if they violate their probation and are sent to prison. The program that is currently sponsored by the Brazoria County Probation Department is only offered to adult probationers who are brought to the Ramsey Unit every other week on a on-time visit. Project Last Chance is an expansion of the program already in existence except that it will be primarily directed towards the recidivist type of juvenile who can be transported to the Unit on a weekly basis to meet with the same inmate regularly. It should be noted that an often heard comment by the adult probationers who are brought to the Unit is that the talks they had with inmates impressed them most. This is the incentive underlining of Project Last Chance: to couple juveniles with veteran inmates in an effort to broaden their horizons and/or wake them up to the rest of their lives".

Change Instead of Chains

Besides Project Last Chance, Dawud developed the idea of getting the message out by means of DVD's meant to reduce recidivism by enlightening the moral conscience of the young men and women who are the most vulnerable in their first adult incarceration. He expects the Departments of Criminal Justice to buy these DVD's from him and show them nationally to first-time offenders between the ages of 17-25 in Self-Help. Pre-Release and Cognitive Intervention Classes in the different correctional facilities.

He made an excellent script, the text of which will be used in the Video. His brochure spells out the basic points the DVD focuses on, which are:

(a) How the multi-dollar entertainment industry glamorizes crime and the so-called underworld, thereby brainwashing the young people into believing it is hip, or in vogue to be a player, thug or thief.

(b) Describes in laymen's terms the three main character traits that all criminals have in common, and how they can rid themselves of such.

(c) Interweaves pro-active affirmations, axioms and incentives throughout the script to elevate their consciences and broaden their horizons and perspectives

(d) Explains in step-by-step detail how the war with self can be conquered, and how it is possible for them to take control of their lives and never again return to prison.

The full wording of the script for the DVD can be found in the Appendix under

On The For Real Side.

These are the words of the last paragraph of the script:
"There are higher roads to travel: roads that are filled with light, so you never have to look over your shoulder. Roads that have no shadows, so you can walk them without shame, roads that are paved with self-respect and honorable accomplishments, roads that lead to heaven.

Do you love your life enough to change it?"

Dawud had excellent feedbacks on the script from various people in and outside the prison. The Imam, the spiritual leader of the Muslim community had this to say: "This is an excellent script for either written or audio/visual. The work is as good if not better than any I've encountered on the subject. Moreover, your personal experience gives it greater validation than others."

Dawud gave me a synopsis of a critique which the warden of the prison, where Dawud then resided, had expressed on three full pages: "Your script is very powerful and dramatic! I believe that it will in fact save the lives of many young men, or at least spare them from what you experienced. If you need my help or endorsement in the future, please feel free to ask." Dawud responded in a letter to me, "I can't think of anything better than saving lives. This realization makes my Spirit Dance!"

The Warden's response means that he would allow Dawud to come into the prison some day with a film crew to film then and there and to conduct interviews with ex-gang members.

In the brochure Dawud announces several other DVD's which are on the drawing board, awaiting funding:

1. Gang Busters (90 min.) which is a strong deterrent against joining a prison and/or a street gang: Live one-on-one interviews with Outlaw Motorcycle, Aryan Brotherhood, Mexican Mafia and Blood ex-gang members from inside the correctional facilities. Each gang member is asked the question: "What is the best advice you would give to a youngster on not joining a gang?"

2. Black Genocide (90 min.) specifically written for young African-American men between the ages of 17-25, because:

   (a) The number one killer of black men in this country between the ages of 17 and 25 is homicide.
   (b) There are more black men in prison than in college.
   (c) Black men have the highest drop-out rate and the lowest G.P.A. at the high school level, even though I.Q. scores parallel one another in all ethnic groups.
   (d) 75% of all black men are raised in single-parent households.

These are all powerful messages which we need, to help turn young people around.

It is a miracle that Dawud has survived all his ordeals and close brushes with death. This must mean that—for a very good reason—he is here so that his story could reach many people.

He needs of course the help of others, of film artists and sponsors, of those who have insight into what a person with that kind of experience can bring. Very few of Dawud's contemporaries, of the people he knew in the past, are still alive. As he expressed so many times: a Guarding Force must have kept his protecting wing over him during all those years.

From my perspective, Love in Action continues, as the celebration of his life will only then be realized when he is allowed to give back to society to its fullest extent.

Chapter Ten

How Do We Know A Person Has Really Changed?

    The answer to this question has been the main reason for writing this book. It was in 2005 that I heard about the execution of Stanley "Tookie" Williams*. I was shocked when I heard the reasons, given by California Governor Arnold Schwarzenegger, which were that *he did not know if Tookie had really changed*. The place: San Quentin prison in San Francisco, the execution date: December 13, 2005. Already very early in his life Tookie was part of the gang scene in South Central, Los Angeles. I visited South Central many times, a place where white people usually don't show up. The neighborhood is a bleak, secondary world, where joblessness is the rule and social life and the economy are ruled by the drug barons. Orland Bishop*, a dear friend of mine, has made a tremendous effort to bring reconciliation between the Crips and the Bloods, the two warring gangs. Tookie was the leader of the Crips. He was charged with fourfold murder, which he denied having committed till the last moment of his life. Tookie spent twenty-five years on death row before finally being executed. Through his many books and his website, he had a tremendous impact on the younger generation in the ghetto. Thousands of young people turned their backs on gang life as could be viewed by their messages on his Website Guest Book. Ten thousand signatures of people demonstrating in his behalf as well as the most influential lawyers speaking in Tookie's behalf, could not change governor Arnold Schwarzenegger's decision not to pardon him. The entire civilized world was disgusted about the fact that one still uses these barbaric methods in America, whereby a person after twenty-five years on death row can still be executed.

The gang problem is huge. In Los Angeles alone there are already 150,000 gang members. That's why it is tragic that someone like Tookie, who was able to reach these young people, was hindered in his peace efforts, and these while he had been nominated four times for the Nobel Peace Prize and three times for the Nobel Prize for Literature. Even President Bush granted him a Prize for Exemplary Volunteer Work with Youth and Gang members involved in criminal activity. Yet, with all this recognition, he still had to die!

Dawud, having been a career criminal, could easily have ended up on death row. That he did not face that same ordeal must be for a good reason, namely, to do, what Tookie was unable to continue, to help young people find their way out of the downward spiral of drugs and gang life. After Dawud's big inner conversion many years ago when he came to an absolute certainty that he never ever wanted to hurt anybody anymore and his decision to find honor with himself, he had already started to have a big impact on first offenders and young inmates in the prison.

Give Him a Chance

In Chapter Eleven I have been explicit about Dawud's deep desire to use his hard won wisdom to help other young people to not go the same route he went in life. He wants to spread the message in the form of DVD's under the heading of:

CHANGE INSTEAD OF CHAINS

He needs, of course, the help of people, of film artists and sponsors, of those who have insight into what a person with that kind of experience can bring. Very few of the contemporaries Dawud knew in the past, are still alive. Many—too many to name them—have ended in violent deaths, in the streets, or in prison. As he expressed so many times: "A Guarding Force must have kept his protecting wing over him during all those years." For what? To just get by somehow?

From my perspective, Love in Action continues, as the celebration of his life will only then be realized when he is allowed to give back to society to its fullest extent.

Seeing the Changes Before They Have Happened

From Goethe we have this important advice:

"If we take people for what they are, we can only make them worse. When we treat them, as if they are already what they should be, we help them on their way, where they want to be."

In order to be successful with this, we need to apply it first to ourselves. Anyone in any place should try to live up to this axiom: the prisoners, the guards, those perpetuating the Criminal Justice System, all of us in society. How we act in society will set the tone for what should happen to those who have stumbled.

How do we know a person has really changed? Ho'oponopono sees the changes before they have happened. I have seen Dawud's ongoing developments, the purification of his soul during the thirty three years I waited for him. I have not only witnessed them, I have also been the person who always believed in Dawud, even when he did not believe in himself. Now he needs the help from more people who recognize his potential as well as realize the urgency of the situation with to-day's young people.

Chapter Eleven

The Spiritual Dimension

Ralph Waldo Emerson once said: "If your circumstances are bothering you, as fast as you can, break off your association with your personal self and identify yourself with the universe. As fast as you can, ignore your 'biographical' self and heed your 'universal' one."

Our world, and especially our present correctional system, could be a very different one if this dimension were practiced in the training of the prison guards. We would be able to give them the tools, first in what thy need for their own development, and then in how to work with this in the prison environment. It holds true for the guards as much as for those incarcerated that the 'low road' needs to meet the 'high road' to bring personal destinies and life into a new balance.

Throughout the pages read so far, the reader may have sensed my belief in inner transformation. This inner transformation is possible for each one of us. Only if we guide our destiny, our life situations, our own soul life, with this an inner certainty, is progress possible. If we are clear about where we came from and where we are going, we would feel less like ships without rudders, tossed about in the wild seas of life. Where do we find guidelines on this path of inner transformation? Where do we find something that can give us inner stability, even in trying times when the old seems to crumble away and we are groping for some new footholds. I have mentioned a few times the names of Rudolf Steiner and Anthroposophy. Rudolf Steiner's insights give clear indications how we can come to inner peace and clarity of mind, while making an active contribution to life and society, be it for us on this side of the walls or for those put away behind walls.

The Anthroposophical Prison Outreach

Those who are incarcerated need the encouragement to take hold of their own life's circumstances and turn them around into a positive direction? Fred Janney, a member of the Anthroposophical Society, who himself worked until recently as a psychologist in Michigan prisons, knew from experience that the message of Anthroposophy was a stabilizing anchor for the many inmates he was counseling. Because inmates are given so little direction on how they can better their lives, he hoped to find people among fellow Anthroposophists, interested in starting an Outreach Program for Prisoners. Rudolf Steiner's attitude on how to view criminal behavior spoke to him. Steiner gives some conditions needed to go an inner path of development in his book *How to Know Higher Worlds**. One of these conditions is that the student should feel himself to be linked to the fabric of all of life. In Rudolf Steiner's own words: "Such an attitude of mind, for instance, alters the way I regard a criminal. I suspend my judgment and say to myself: 'I am like him, only a human being. Through favorable circumstances I received an education, which perhaps alone saved me from a similar fate'. I may also come to the conclusion that this human brother of mine would have become a different man had my teachers taken the same pains with him they took with me. I shall reflect on the fact that something was given to me which was withheld from him, that I enjoy my fortune precisely because it was denied him. And then I shall naturally come to think of myself as a link in the whole of humanity and a sharer in the responsibility for everything that occurs."

This insight led to the birth of the Anthroposophical Prison Outreach, the mission of which is focused on *strengthening human bonds between individuals separated by prison walls through the medium of Anthroposophy as a path of inner and social development.* The Anthroposophical Prison Outreach (APO) has been providing introductory packets for prisoners. Inmates can then request to borrow books from the library (free of charge) on topics like meditation, spiritual development, intuitive thinking as a spiritual path among many other titles. In the APO Newsletter, which is distributed four times a year to the inmates, who have requested these materials, as well as to the sponsors of this program, worthwhile articles about such topics are discussed. Inmates also share their experiences with the exercises, give book reports and share their poetry and art work. A few examples chosen from the many who wrote back and gave positive feedback on the program and the help they received follow:

"My pain and shame is deeply embedded in my bloodstream for I see now the negative life I chose to live in opposition to the positive role I could have taken. And so I can feel the wounds still that have carried me to seek *knowledge of the purpose and meaning of life* so as to come full circle and not only to find myself at its higher level but find the very essence of life, love and gratitude towards all."

"You speak to me from the teachings Steiner created. Isn't that amazing? Reaching all the way into the depths of madness to find and inspire me, not give up on me, my hidden potential, and the beauty which is within me."

Many prisoners have subscribed to the correspondence course EduCareDo, a Self Awakening Study Course in Anthroposphy—Spiritual Science (again, free of charge). As one inmate wrote: "I feel blessed to have had this year of study through EduCareDo to add understanding, insight and momentum to live this life."

Through these and other contents people are addressed, not as inmates or numbers, but in their dignity as human beings. Good tidings spread around quickly in what could be called a wasteland of human potential. The number of packets sent to inmates in every state runs into the hundreds. In some prisons volunteers, familiar with the ideas of Anthroposophy, may work regularly with a group of inmates, which has formed around him or her. One volunteer told how he went in with some trepidations and fear, but found that the experience did not match in any way his apprehension. Quite the opposite, "The men were so generous and warm, friendly even. I wondered what all my fear had been about. I also realized that our culture created this fear." Many inmates have also entered into a correspondence with Anthroposophists.

A New Approach for Juvenile Offenders

How does this uplifting of the individual relate to the major changes that could come about in the system? The debate in health care is aware of the fact that prevention is more satisfying and cost cutting than any other approach.

In the same way we can look at the real changes needed for effective work with young people at risk. A true success story needs to be shared here about the work done with the Waldorf educational curriculum with juvenile offenders and kids on probation in Marysville, California. The Juvenile Hall is a maximum security lock-up facility. At night the young people are locked up in cells, but in day time they go to school. What made this school so special is that the principal, Ruth Mikkelsen, was able to inspire the teachers to embark on a whole new approach in education. The teachers, who went through many Waldorf Teacher Training sessions at the Rudolf Steiner College*, were baffled by all the new things they had to learn themselves, before they could pass them on to the pupils, such as story telling, singing, playing the recorder, painting with water colors, drawing and integrating the arts into academic lessons. What touched the young people more than anything else was story telling. By presenting the lessons orally students, who initially had a deep aversion to reading and writing, were inwardly engaged and began to forge a positive connection to school and learning. In Juvenile Hall first thing in the morning students would ask, "Are we getting a story?" When the teacher told one, there was total attention. *One boy who was scheduled for a court appearanc, asked his probation officer if he could go first so he would be back in time for the story.* At Parents Day, at the end of the first year of this innovative program, two fifteen year old boys played a Mozart duet on their recorders. It was a miracle that these boys, who had been part of rival gangs, were able to do this. They had been expelled from public school for violent acts, constant failure in class and refusal to follow directions. It definitely was the arts, and, specifically, the music through singing and learning to play an instrument, which caught the interest of the young people. When they came to Juvenile Hall they had an aversion to school, but, slowly, they really got interested and excited about it Here is what one of the students said, after having been part of this program for some time: "I like all the arts. For example recorder class. I have learned how to read music. And my wood-burning class had a great reward! I won first place in a contest. The contest made me feel I can accomplish anything I put my mind to. The singing is fun. It really brings out the vocalist in all of us". This student had failed every public school program he ever attended. Via the arts and music the students also became interested in the other subjects, especially as these were now brought in an artistic and lively manner. *The success was so great that some of the young people asked the judge to extend their sentences, as they preferred to stay in school and learn more, instead of being cast out again onto the mean streets.*

The Rudolf Steiner College in Fair Oaks, California, continues to do Teacher Training in two week summer intensives where teachers learn how to work with young people at risk.

The T.E.Matthews Court School and the Juvenile Hall in Marysville, California, fit exactly with my experiences, working with inner city youths in summer programs in Chicago. The wildest kids would become lambs, absorbing the stories like sponges, often even while starting to suck their thumbs. Much of public school teaching does not reach the core of young people. Their inner soul lives are not enriched, dry out and shrivel up. Most of the time they get "stones instead of bread".

Waiting for Dawud

Am I still waiting for Dawud? Is he still waiting for me? Yes, we are. We all are somewhere on a path of development. Some start in the darkness of the dungeons, some come floating down on wings of light. Some learn waiting in the work with handicapped children, others wait while a parent succumbs to Alzheimers, soldiers wait to ambush the enemy; a mother waits nine months for her child to be born. Waiting can be a very active process, waiting can also be called "life in action".

For a long time I was worried that I could be a helpful companion to only one person, Dawud.

What about all the other people, still languishing away, who do not have any support to show them that there is another way? It took me a while to understand that something happens for all people and connects all living beings, when even one person is able to make the radical shift of change from being a career criminal to becoming a person who wants to share his hard-won inner gold. I am sure there are many, many such stories of inner transformation. Yes, only one at a time, but with a cumulative effect on all those who are becoming true, striving, human beings.

Let us try to imagine the new world in the making when we learn to live in accordance with the high aims our Maker has set out for us. Emerson expresses this in a beautiful way:

"A Breath of Will blows Eternally through the Universe of Souls in the Direction of the Right and the Necessary"

APPENDIX

About Being Honest With Yourself

"Take God into your actions of Will and
He will descend form heaven."

(Schiller)

This title suggests that being honest with yourself is more important than being honest with the external world. Of course, both sides are interconnected, but usually, the emphasis is on the connection with the outside world rather than with oneself. Here, however, I want to direct your attention towards communication with oneself. The title suggests also, that "I" and "Self" are two different things: "I" am honest with my "Self".

We all know about the two souls which are constantly in conflict within ourselves: part of the soul is directed by and to the outside world in terms of "What impression do I make on other people?" or "What do people think of me?" The other voice from within, which usually knows better, knows what I am *really* supposed to do.

Many of you will know from experience that you can try to silence this inner voice for a long time, but in times of disaster—injury, hospitalization, arrest, solitary confinement—it will be with you and overpower, by its inner strength, all other considerations. Such a moment can awaken us to the realization, that we want to accomplish something good in the world, and that we want to be our true selves, and not what others expect us to be. At such a moment, we can be at one with the inner goal of our life and see the meaning of our existence.

Is there a way, a path to follow, an active direction to take, in order to be able to stay in touch with this inner voice? Or, when the pain of the injury has subsided, when the shock of the arrest has passed, or when we are taken from solitary confinement back to the general population—will we again succumb to the influence and demands of the external world and its people?

Many people are bored and disgusted with life as it presents itself; they are paralyzed by their feeling of powerlessness. This is how a young man expressed himself: "Against all deficiencies of our time like fear, suicidal attitudes, loneliness, the immobility and decadence, there is only one remedy: one's own Ego, which by its own force has embarked on a serious journey of schooling one's thoughts and of cultivating one's inner life." *

(From ":Steps to Freedom" by Albert Reps)

Thus, from the very start, the most active positive direction a person can take is to ask: "When did I hear this inner voice? What did it tell me? Did I live up to it?" To ask these questions is the first task to fulfill. When the real goal becomes clear, one can begin to walk the path which leads to that goal. In order for this idea not to remain a vague wish, one has to connect one's will with it. We have to act, to put the resolve into a deed. It is, therefore, necessary to create a practice schedule for conversing with one's self; that is, to set aside a time during which the world around you is reasonably quiet, like the moment before going to sleep or the moment after waking up in the morning. Of course, we should not scold ourselves or let any feelings of guilt or inadequacy enter the soul if it is hard to focus on this. Rather one should trust the idea that one's real self knows what is good and what needs to be done in order to bring to life this goodness within us and in others. By practicing this conversation with Self, one has the chance on a regular basis, to get in touch with the seeds of goodness in oneself. It will take a long time and an enormous amount of effort, but then the time can come when all of one's thoughts and feelings will be permeated with this new reality. It can bring a feeling of inner peace, a feeling that you really possess the tools to manage your own life, and are not just chaotically driven like a boat tossed around on the ocean of circumstances.

The inner peace, obtained as a result of communicating with Self, can gradually penetrate all the waking hours of the day. There are some dangers, namely that another superficial "self" creep into one's existence. One way of checking, if one is in touch with one's real self as supposed to the more superficial layer of the soul, is to see whether this self wants to exist by separating itself from the rest of the world, or whether one feels basically in harmony with the totality of existence. Only if the latter case is true, will you know that you are on the right path.

The better we manage to be honest with ourselves, the better we will be able to be honest with other people. For example: in dealing with one's children, one will never promise something which one is unable to keep. Because, if you look at your own life, this is perhaps what happened to you. You may have started to distrust people because you were often not given what was promised to you. However, the tide can be turned, if you decide to do so.

Being honest is being in touch with one's own truth which is part of the greater Truth. Honesty is a key part of the process of living up to it. Honesty has a much larger meaning than only "not lying". Honesty, as it is referred to here, means taking the truth of your own existence into your daily life, independent of the environment in which you are at this very moment.

-.-.-.-.-.-.-

Viktor Frankl

"There is nothing conceivable, that would so condition
a man, as to leave him without the slightest freedom"

(Viktor Frankl)

Viktor Frankl has written "The Will to Meaning"
about his experiences in prison. In World War II, Viktor
Frankl was for years imprisoned by the Nazis in the
Auschwitz concentration camp on the mere grounds
that he belonged to the Jewish race. In the camp, those
prisoners who were able-bodied, and were not chosen
for extermination immediately, were forced to do hard
labor from dawn to dusk, such as digging ditches, laying
railroad tracks, or felling trees.

All this was under the most severe conditions: having
completely inadequate shoes and clothing while working
in sub-zero temperatures, hardly any food to sustain
strength and no medical care. The prisoners worked under
constant thread of torture and violence.

We can ask how it could be possible that a man who
has survived such an experience could still speak of
freedom? What beliefs could he have held? What were
the choices he made?

- He could believe that he indeed was an outcast of
  society, because of his race OR he could realize
  that an aberration of thought had taken hold
  of an entire nation (Germany) to promote such

terrible racism and know that, despite this, our true human nature has nothing to do with race.

- He could have succumbed to the circumstances and become like an animal, fighting and grabbing for every crumb of food he could get hold of OR he could keep standards of decent human behavior.
- He could curry favors, betraying fellow prisoners by collaborating with the oppressors in order to get cigarettes or some extra food rations OR he could keep his pride in upholding human dignity, even though he had to endure more suffering.

Viktor Frank knew where he wanted to stand as a man. He knew that he always had to keep the flame of hope alive within him. He fought to learn to see *meaning* in all his experience. He saw that even there where the depths of the human soul had been ripped open, there was the same pattern: there was good and bad in the prisoners, there was good and bad in the guards. And that good and bad was bound in a unity together.

Imprisonment in the United States is not as extreme as these experiences. Yet it is similar in that one's freedom is taken away. What are the tools needed to be able to have a degree of freedom even within this state of captivity?

1. The first is knowing that your spirit *can never be imprisoned,* because it is not of the physical / material world.
2. Understanding of your situation in terms of the causes of imprisonment which lie in you, lie in society, and in the interaction between you and the world.

It is the power of thinking, real thinking, that can bestow on us a certain inner freedom. I do not speak here of the necessity of occupying yourself with law books and legal matters, or with all the media and channels that are necessary to stay in contact with the outer world, no, I am talking about **Creative Thinking** that starts to see the real connections in the world. It turns around the usual patterns of thought:

"The most securely imprisoned population that exists is the general public that is uninformed about the nature and the consequences of imprisonment as practiced in a mass delusion, which in the long run punishes society far more severely than society can ever punish a convicted criminal."

*Hans Mattick**

Real insight does not put the blame on anything or anyone. It only tries to restore, to reconcile.

In our day-to day dealing with prison personnel and other prisoners, we have the freedom to ignore the other person's real self or to address it in each new instance, adding or taking away from the real human substance that weaves between people.

This process of inner freedom through **creative thinking** can only function when one accepts also the solitude of isolation from others. The great architect, Louis Sullivan, wrote at the end of his life, "This solitude of isolation from others is necessary for the development of man's identity. And everyone, who will become truly creative, must find within himself his own individual selfhood. He may find there a dungeon or a limitless universe, according to the use the individual is willing to make of his own faculties."

This is the inner freedom that can be gained in prison and anywhere else.

Accept the solitude of isolation
Through it the insight can arise that my Ego,
my "I", my higher Self,
is part of the limitless Universe and the
universal Meaning
for all that happens in this world.

Out of this insight I can have the realization that each person I meet has

33 Ways to Play a Loser's Game

by David Anglin-Bullis
(written in 1980, in Jackson Prison)

Crime is a loser's game for most, and just the appellation of the word Criminal to you may well cause your family and friends untold anguish, starting with the lead-in of arrest and into jail, the eventually pleas-bargaining or trial. It's all downhill from there. Errant individuals convicted of felonies and ticketed for prison ought to know that the following list of unpleasantries await them behind tall massive penitentiary walls.

1. First of all, expect to be stranded in prison for a while, and maybe for many, long, trying, lonesome years.
2. If you have to be in prison for over three or four years, expect to lose contact with some or all of your family and former so-called friends.
3. Don't expect anyone to agree with "your notion" of justice, nor will some miracle come along that will instantaneously affect your release.
4. Don't expect too soon if ever to win a reversal from any higher court or appeal. The vast majority of imprisoned persons lose their appeals consistently.
5. There will be absolutely no privacy, and you can expect to do "hard time" in a hostile environment.
6. Don't expect the twisted circumstances of imprisonment in themselves to improve anyone's character or disposition. Since association is forced and limited by the very nature of the prison

situation some of your companions will oscillate between explosive bad temper and boisterous annoyance. Others will unapproachably withdraw to the point of being totally uncommunicative.

7. In Prison we have been thrust into an abnormal twilight zone where neurosis, psychosis and paranoia reign supreme. You are to be pitied if you expect any meaningful interest in you or your problems.

8. Expect no compassion, love, or sympathy from your fellow prisoners or from your keepers.

9. There will undoubtedly be overcrowding, continuous backbiting and endless gossip out of which all kinds of wild rumors will come. What little fact and truth is circulated around in prison is unfortunately mangled by most prisoners.

10. Expect the 6 x 9 cell, that will be your home, to be filthy, your bed, graced with a dirty mattress, will be ancient and one or more of your fixtures: electricity (lights), sink or toilet, may not work.

11. The majority of the time you will have to wear prison issued ill-fitting perma-wrinkle clothing, that will always be in short supply. The scuffed shoes you will be given may have been worn by ten more men before you.

12. Every door (and there are many) will be securely locked, and the food will be terrible.

13. There is continual confusion in prison, loud discordant noises from morning to night, and often vermin-mice, rats, flies, mosquitoes, roaches and an abundance of other sundry insects.

14. There will be an interminable wait for anything and everything and your incoming mail will be read before you get it, no matter what official

claims to the contrary. Everyone in authority, administrators and guards, habitually lies to prisoners. Prisoners can also be expected to lie regularly.

15. Little respect, honor or integrity is to be found in prison, but discourtesy and dishonesty or petty theft are common-pace occurrences.

16. Every imprisoned individual will have his own unique sad tale to tell, and most prisoners will at least make a claim of "technical innocence".

17. There are hundreds of written and unwritten rules that attempt to govern your in-prison behavior, but don't expect any everyday guidance. There are no set criteria, specific steps or programs for making parole, and no logical or reasonable explanations are going to be given for anything.

18. Monotony, regimentation—sameness—will characterize your existence, so you may expect to experience the depths of frustration.

19. You will be hustled, jostled, and manipulated from every conceivable angle, and you can expect half of the prisoners you meet to be armed with some kind of crude weapon.

20. Whimsical transfers from one prison to another are frequent; and there will be little or no association with the opposite sex.

21. Expect rampant homosexuality, brutality (physical and psychological), vicious prison politics, concentrated in the hands of a few concerned with the preservation of their own special privileges for the most part, and there will also be a plethora of non-political tight-knit cliques, none of which will welcome you.

22. Without going out of your way in the least, you can count on violating one or more of the prison's many rules and regulations. A punishment of some sort will surely follow.

23. Kites to the warden, counselors or other administrative personnel will be tersely answered in a condescending way in a matter of days—if you're lucky.

24. Where you perceive some unfairness or wrong, and individually or collectively seek redress through petition via mail to any official of the department of corrections in the state's capitol, expect disappointment, a flat rejection of your allegations or contentions.

25. You will have no "rights", so don't delude yourself into thinking that you do.

26. You will hear guards and prisoners applying derogatory terms to all races and ethnic groups. There will be guard harassments, and in disputes between guards and prisoners, the prisoner invariably loses.

27. There will be days when you won't be able to get essentials, like official forms you may need for various purposes.

28. Showers ill be in an unsanitary area, where the water will always be too hot or too cold, and more than likely you won't be supplied with a washcloth or towel.

29. The sheets on your bed will often be torn or raggedy, and they will seldom be the size of your mattress.

30. Bacterial and viral epidemics periodically plague prisons, so expect to catch whatever is going around.

31. Don't expect the best if any in dental or medical care.
32. Expect prison so-called clergy to sanction by silence official and unofficial prison policy, no matter how inhumane.
33. Don't be fooled into thinking that prison can be likened to a small harmonious community or society. There will be little or no unity of purpose, and your aims and goals probably won't coincide with those of anyone else.

Who are the Chosen Ones?

Russian Legend by Alexej Remisow

There is in the world divine a light clear paradise—
the holy realm of the angels.
Illumined by celestial light, there stands the city
of the chosen ones—
and their guardian is the almighty angel:
Made out of light is his bright clear garment,
extended are his white shining wings,
and he is holding the sword in his hands.

Over there golden apples are the joy of the righteous
ones, together with the sirens
they are singing well-sounding songs, and are
comforting the holy and pious ones.
There is no sadness or sighing, there is eternal life.

Troublesome and long is the road, that leads
to the holy paradise.
Many are called to join the meal in this holy place,
but the holy light was never enjoyed by those
who were not chosen.
They did not reach the boundary stone: because of the
angel, the mighty guardian:

Made out of light is his bright clear garment,
extended are his white shining wings
and he is holding the sword in his hands.

To whom then are open the gates of paradise?
And who are the chosen ones among all those,
who are called?
—a pure heart, that is committed in trying to do God's
will,—that is chosen By God;
—a heart, which through suffering and trying has
exhausted itself,—that is chosen by God;
—a wounded heart,—that is chosen by God;
—a heart that is open to human misery and distress,
that is chosen by God;
—a heart that can bring joy and blessing as well,
—that is chosen by God;
—a heart that is humble,—that is chosen by God;
—a heart that, offended, almost consumed itself for grief;
—that is chosen by God;
—a heart that was inflamed for the sake of truth,
—that was chosen by God;
—a heart that tormented itself for our veracity,
—that is chosen by God;
—a heart that is gentle,—that is chosen by God;
—a heart that is willing to take on even the greatest sin
for the sake of the divine light, for the sake of purity
on this toilsome earth in the cruel world,
—that is chosen by God;
—the great heart of the Mother of the light—the Star
among stars;—which wanted to go with us, the ones that
are doomed to death,
—that is a heart,—that is chosen by God,—

TO THIS ONE THE GATES OF PARADISE ARE
OPEN.

Dr. Quackenbush Psychological Report

UTMB Correctional Managed Health Care
Mental Health Services—Ramsey—Retrieve Units

To whom it may concern: Re: Bullis, David
                                        TDCJ # 488301

At the request of the above mentioned inmate this report will summarize his treatment by the Psychiatric Services Department, changes he has made and his current status

Inmate Bullis presented me in June 1992 with concerns about understanding himself and his long term pattern of criminal behaviors. At that time he requested counseling to "find out what's going on with me? .... I'm angry at myself." His stated goal was to attempt to change his negative orientation and behaviors through therapy and the development of self understanding. He was then enrolled in individual therapy and he has been seen on a regular basis for almost five years.

This inmate who was a career criminal, having spent over 20 years incarcerated since the age of sixteen, demonstrated positive motivation for change at a level which was unusual when compared with others with whom I have worked over the past ten years. He developed insight into his problems and he became aware of the nature and consequences of his criminal behaviors. Of critical importance is that he does not blame others for his problems and accepts full responsibility for his actions. In addition, he has developed strong victim empathy and now seeks ways in which he could pay back to society for his past criminal actions.

During the past five years. He has worked through several periods of F associated with his development of guilt and shame as well as in response to negative events in his environment, such as receiving a set-off, and during times in which he was not progressing rapidly enough in his personal growth.

One of the ways he has expressed a changed attitude is in his work with young offenders who are on probation and who are brought to the prison unit in an attempt to give them some appreciation of what might happen to them if they violate their probation. He speaks with these individuals on a one-to-one basis and apparently has had some success in reaching them emotionally and being a positive influence on their thinking. He feels that he understands these young people better than others might, as he says "I see myself at age sixteen and I know what happened to me."

In clinical terms it is felt that he has made consistent and positive gains in resolving the psychological issues which were contributing to his criminal behavior. It is also important that he has continued in his therapy and has had a significant and has had a significant amount of time to consolidate those gains which increases the chance that his changed thinking and behavior has now become a part of his behavioral patterns. It is felt that these changes are the most important as criminal behavior comes from criminal thinking patterns and the most successful programs are those which focus on the criminal thinking patterns.

In review of current mental status this individual is not depressed and not experiencing perceptual or cognitive dysfunction. His reality ties are strong, his thinking processes are organized and directed towards positive goals. Maintenance therapy is now offered to consolidate gains and to maintain the positive already achieved.

John F. Quackenbush, Ph.D   May 1, 1002
                                    Correctional Psychologist

Autobiographical Sketch

by David Anglin-Bullis

Regardless of how dark you think the dungeon is, be it actual or imagined, there's a light within you that can never be extinguished. I'm able to say this with considerable authority, having spent over twenty-seven years (half of my life) in prison.

I began this odyssey in 1965 by being sent to an adult prison, when I was sixteen, because I told the police I was seventeen, not wanting to be returned to Juvenile Hall from where I had escaped. The main reason I didn't want to return, was because there was a young attendant there who I was dreadfully afraid of. He used to come into my room at night and beat me severely all over my body with one of my gym shoes. These beatings were so vicious, they were sadistic in nature and the most savage I had ever received in my entire life. But even though I was black and blue and had welts for a week afterwards, they did not curtail my wild and mischievous nature.

Prior to my arrest I was raised in the all American dysfunctional family. Both my mother and stepfather were alcoholics and emotionally retarded. As role models they did not possess any redeeming quality that I wanted to emulate. To this day I can't remember a single conversation I had with either of them in which they even made a half-hearted attempt to enlighten my conscience, or steer me in a positive direction. Just to say that they allowed me to do whatever I damn well pleased, would be an understatement.

When I was eleven, because of excessive truancies, multiple thief charges And Repeated run-aways from home, the Juvenile Court intervened and switched primary custody to my real father. In 1960 I went to live with him and his new family: my stepmother, who was in her late twenties, step brother who was five and step sister, who was three. They lived in a quaint neighborhood right from the pages of Life magazine, which to me was on the other side of the galaxy from the inner city where I had grown up in.

I fell in love with my stepmother overnight, as she was charming, smart as a whip and had a delightful sense of humor. She became my first real friend and was ten times the mother to me than my real mother ever was. My father worked the evening shift, so throughout the week I would only see him during supper. Although he was a man of few words and a firm disciplinarian, he had a gentle loving sprit and to this day I cannot think of one bad thing to say about him.

I lived with them for three and a half years, and it was the closest I have ever experienced to having a normal childhood. When I reflect back how they tried and tried till their hearts were almost busted to straighten out a wild boy's life, it was to no avail as I was already too far gone before I went ot live with them. They took me to a child psychologist, who said he could find no psychosis, but he believed I practically had no conscience.

When I was fourteen, my father took me back into the inner city to live with my mother, because my uncontrollable behavior had become too much to deal with. I spent the next two years in and out of Juvenile Hall, running the streets and gang banging.

The charge that took me to prison the first time was Armed Robbery, for which O received five years. Back in the mid-sixties, Ionia Reformatory in Northern Michigan, was a brutal, eerie place, but even though I was the youngest inmate there, I quickly blended right in with the other misfits and hooligans. I got into a fight every day for the first three days and got my severely whipped, but I had passed muster, proving that I had heart; therefore I was accepted into the fraternal order of the Brotherhood of the Damned.

I was paroled nineteen months later. In retrospect of my first sentence, what stand out in my

Memory more than anything else, was that when I got released in '67, I was more criminally minded, and twice as violent and aggressive than when I went in. During the next three years I spent almost all of it in prison, violating my parole twice. Within this time frame I developed a ferocious appetite for fine literature. Fortunately, I had at my disposal one of the best libraries in northern Michigan, because some wealthy entrepreneur had donated his private library to the prison when he died. Considering that my reading comprehension, spelling and vocabulary was only at grade school level, it still baffles me to this day what compelled me to start reading the "classics" at that stage of my life. Another factor which made my reading interest so strange, was that all my peers were reading nothing but main stream books: Murder Mysteries, Science Fiction and Westerns. I'm not going to list all the really great books that I read during that era, but when I was in my mid-forties I came across a list of one hundred greatest books ever written, which was complied by a prominent panel of literature professors. Surprisingly I had read over thirty of them by the time I was nineteen.

The one book that stands out in my memory above them all was <u>Man's Search for Meaning"</u> by Viktor Frankl. I had discovered it by chance, as I had developed a keen interest in the holocaust. This book, more than any other, would prove to have a dramatic influence upon my life.

In 1970 I was arrested for second degree murder, stemming from a robbery that had gotten out of hand. At my trial eleven months later I was found guilty of manslaughter and sentenced to ten to fifteen years.

I was twenty-one when I arrived at the State Prison of Southern Michigan in May 1971. Little did I know that I was entering a world where all my nightmares would come true, and I would witness and experience (like Dr. Frankl) man's cruelty in the extreme. During the mid-seventies, Jackson Prison had the highest murder rate of any prison in America. That's because it was wide open. Gambling was legal and drugs of every variety were plentiful. I started smoking weed in '73 on a regular basis which progressed to smoking it every day for the next five years. Although I experimented with LSD, heroine and amphetamine, weed was my drug of choice during this time frame

I have often been asked what it was like to have lived in an environment where I witness almost on a daily occurrence: men brutally stabbed and bludgeoned to death, thrown from the fourth tier (floor) of a cell block, burned to a cinder in a locked cell and savagely gang raped. I tell them that if they can imagine being on the front line during a fire fight, then that would be a fair similarity. In retrospect, the only explanation I can give for having survived those extremely wild and violent years (at least physically), was that I must have a very powerful angel protecting me; considering that, I was just as involved—more or less—in the prison's subculture, which caused me to have several life and death confrontations with my peers.

After enduring eight years of this horror, I was transferred to a trusty camp, where I escaped shortly thereafter.

Two and a half days later I was apprehended with a pistol. Consequently I had five years added to my sentence.

Even though I had been raised catholic, I was light years away from being a spiritual person. Actually, I was a hard core agnostic, leaning towards atheism. When I was returned back inside the prison, this belief was drastically altered, as I embraced Islam and became a Muslim.

Again, in retrospect, I now clearly understand why my belief paradigm underwent such a radical change. It is typical for men in prison to fervently reach out to any ideology that will alleviate their emotional stress. In other words, prison by its mere design, is a relentless monster that will steadily and silently eat away at your humanity, and render you gasping for anything that will relieve this starvation.

In 1980 I met and married shortly thereafter a Dutch Eurythmist. Besides having the same day and month birth date, we had so many other things in common, that she believed that we were twins in another life. Not only did she become my best friend (and remains so to this day), she also became my mentor and point of reference from which I measure the real nature of things, as she is, by far, the truest and most human person I have ever known.

In May 1981 I was released from prison after serving eleven consecutive years. Seven months later I had my parole transferred to Texas. In '83 I got involved with another woman who became pregnant. Regretfully, I got a divorce and married her. My daughter, Khadija, was born shortly thereafter.

From '81 to '96 I had no contact with the authorities. I had "squared up" so to speak. During those five years I graduated from Chef School and went on to serve a three year apprenticeship, working in some of the top restaurants in Houston. In that year (1986) I had risen to the top of my profession, as I was working in the capacity of Executive Chef at a prestigious yacht club in Galveston; unfortunately, I was using cocaine and weed heavily. One night in a drug induced stupor, I ran off with the club's cash revenue. Three days later I was arrested in New Orleans on charges of: attempted capital murder of a police officer, possession of a firearm, and possession of a controlled substance. All of these charges were later reduced to a misdemeanor, because a glitch that appeared on the computer, when they ran a N.C.S.C (felony back ground check) on me. After serving seven months in the Parish prison, I was extradited back to Texas, where I received five years for the theft from the yacht club. After serving another seven months I was paroled.

During the fourteen months my wife divorced me. A year later we were reconciled had started living together. Shortly thereafter she pressed charges against me for sexual assault, to which I pled guilty and received twenty-five years for. Because of my criminal history I was sent to the Michael's Unit, which was one of the most dangerous prisons in Texas. The events which stand out in my memory more than any other were: within the first ten days that I was there three inmates were murdered. I met a real Klan's man (member of the Ku Klux Klan), who revealed to me the extensive anti-government and extremely racist underground that is flourishing in this country. And even though I had religiously participated in Narcotics Anonymous all the while I was there, within hours after I was released I was shooting up cocaine.

The reason hat I ended up serving only three years on a twenty-five years sentence, was because my ex-wife had written to me and said that she forgave me as she felt what happened was a crime of passion. It was her letter, which I showed to the Parole Board, that won my release.

I only stayed out two and a half months, whereupon I picked up a new eighteen year sentence for burglary of an auto. The court ran it concurrently with the twenty-two years I had left from my original sentence, so when I returned to prison, I was classified as a parole violator with a new sentence. I doubt very seriously if I can describe the state of mind I was in when I returned to prison this time, except to say that it was the absolute lowest point of my life. I once heard someone say, "You can't begin to raise up until you have hit rock bottom." Well, I had crashed into some fathomless pit that would take me years to even get back to the surface, let alone straighten out a life that wasn't worth a farthing.

Carlos the Caterpillar

By David A. Anglin-Bullis

Chapter One: The Awakening

It was a bright and clear summer morning. There were giant marshmallow clouds playing tag and follow the leader in the crystal blue sky over the border town of Del Rio.

The birds, nature's alarm clock, were singing their cheerful good morning to each other, and the sun was smiling down upon the little vegetable garden behind Rebecca Sanchez's house.

Carlos, who had spent the night curled up warm and snugly inside the petals of a yellow daffodil, had just awakened. His very first thought on this brand new day was of food, as he was always hungry, but it wasn't because he was greedy or selfish. He just somehow knew he had to prepare himself for that magical day when he would spin his cocoon, and sleep in it the whole winter, and then in the spring come out of it as a beautiful Monarch butterfly.

While he was crawling down the stem of the daffodil, little did he know that he wasn't the only one with breakfast on his mind. Perched high in the branches of an elm tree at the back of the garden sat Paco the raven, and with his very sharp eyes he saw Carlos climbing down and thought, "That fat little caterpillar sure would make a tasty meal." So he quickly took flight, swooping towards the unsuspecting Carlos on silent wings. When he was just about to snatch Carlos, there came a loud bang from the back porch and Rebecca came bouncing down the steps carrying a water can. The surprise noise of the screen door made slamming shut so scared Paco that he let out a frightened cry. When Carlos heard Paco scream, he quickly rolled into a small ball and hid himself under a fallen rose leaf. Having missed his prey, Paco flew to a nearby fence post and angrily squawked at Rebecca. When she heard Paco squawking, she shook her fist a him and said,

"One of these days I'm going to have to take my shotgun to that pesky black crow!"

For many years Rebecca and Paco had been feuding because every spring when she planted her vegetable garden, he would sneak behind her back and steal as many of the freshly planted seeds that he could without being caught. Paco wasn't really a mean or bad sort of bird, but he was always playing pranks on someone or getting into some type of mischief in the neighborhood. Maybe this was why no one liked him and he had no friends to play with. Paco was very lonely.

When Carlos thought it was safe to come out from hiding, he crawled from under the leaf and up onto the rose bush and started munching away on the tasty leaves to his heart's content. While eating, he saw Rebecca watering all the pretty flowers and thought, "I wonder why she only talks to the flowers and not to the other plants and vegetables in her garden. Doesn't she know that they can all hear her too?"

When Rebecca reached the rose bush and saw Carlos eating on it, she gently picked him up and held him in the palm of her hand and said, "So you're the little rascal that's been eating all the leaves off my rose bush, well we can't have that." So she carried him over to the fence and sat him down on the other side of it. At first Carlos was a bit scared, as he had never been out of the garden before, but he decided to make the best of the situation and started looking around for something else to eat.

While he was looking about he heard someone singing in the most beautiful voice he had ever heard. The song was so beautiful that it seemed to pull him towards it as if a spell had been cast over him. Looking upwards, he realized that the song was coming from high over his head, so he started crawling up the stem of the giant sunflower. Up and up he crawled, and the higher he climbed the more beautiful the song became. When he reached the top of the sunflower he was able to see who was singing. Carlos had never seen such a strange looking insect before. It was brown and furry and had eight long legs and sat in the middle of what looked like a net made of very thin white thread that was stretched between the stems of two tall sun flowers. Carlos thought, "I must talk to this insect, maybe he'll teach me how to sing so beautifully." When Carlos was just about to step onto the spider's web he heard someone below him shout, "If you step onto Luigi's web it will probably the last step you ever take!" Carlos looked down and there, hovering in midair was the largest blue and green dragonfly Carlos had ever seen. Just then he turned and saw Luigi racing towards him stepping nimbly over the strands of his web. When he saw Luigi's fangs bared, with a very hungry expression on his face, he became so frightened that he couldn't move a muscle in his body. Again he heard the dragonfly shout, "Hurry and jump onto my back caterpillar before it is too late!" Realizing that he didn't have a second to spare, Carlos shut his eyes, held his breath and jumped onto the dragonfly's back and they quickly flew out of harm's way.

Flying to a nearby pond, they landed on a large lily pad. As soon as Carlos crawled of the dragonfly's back, he introduced himself and said, "Thank you, kind sir, for saving my life." The dragonfly gracefully bowed to Carlos and said, "Please allow me to introduce myself. My name is Nathaniel, and your gratitude humbles my heart, but you need not thank me, for I am a Knight of the Forest, and it is my sworn duty to protect all living beings and to defend the laws of nature."

Carlos could hardly believe his ears, let alone his eyes. For most of his life he had been hearing stories about these famous knights and their heroic deeds from the other insects and animals in the garden, but no one he knew had ever actually seen one.

It was Carlos' habit to be curious about everything. He said to Nathaniel, "Sir knight, would you please tell me what a Knight of the Forest is, and what are the laws of nature you are sworn to defend?"

"I'll answer both of your questions, if you first tell me why you want to know these things, but you must speak from the heart." Carlos did not quite know what Nathaniel meant by speaking from the heart, "I guess he means to speak the truth," so he thought for a while, then said' "I've been looking for something meaningful to devote my life to when I grow older, and becoming a Knight of the Forest sounds like a noble path to pursue."

That indeed was a very good answer, as it tells me that you are wise beyond your years," Nathaniel said, "But you must always remember this, just to say you want something is meaningless because it doesn't matter what you say, it only matters what you do. Now then, I'm going to explain to you what a true knight is, so play close attention. First and foremost, a Knight of the Forest is someone who has dedicated his life to the Supreme Spirit. In his service, a knight defends the four basic laws of nature the Supreme Spirit has given us to live a righteous and honorable life by. These laws are: not to murder, steal from, lie to, or harm in any manner another living being. This I can assure you is not an easy path to follow. In fact, of al the paths in the world to choose from, this one is by far the most difficult."

"If you knew it was going to be so difficult, why did you choose it Nathaniel?"

"I chose it because I know beyond a shadow of a doubt that it's the path which leads to heaven."

Listening to Nathaniel' deep words of wisdom, and staring at the goodness that was in his eyes, Carlos knew that Nathaniel was a very special being, and he wondered if he, a mere caterpillar, could one day become a Knight of the Forest just like him?

"Sir knight, I know that I'm only a caterpillar, but would you please tell me if I might be able to become a knight one day?"

"That's not a decision I only can make. Only the Council of Knights in Queen Victoria's forest can vote someone into the knighthood, and only a knight can recommend someone to the council."

'What would I have to do for you to recommend me, Nathaniel?"

"First of all, you would have to become my squire and pledge your allegiance to me. Then you would have to prove your honor and worthiness for me to recommend you. Once you take your pledge, it will be my sworn duty to teach you the rules of conduct all knights must live by."

"When can we begin, Nathaniel?"

"We'll begin as soon as I return from a mission I must make to the other side of the forest. While I'm gone, you'll be taking a test of character. I know that caterpillars can't swim, therefore, it will be your challenge to use your smarts and your courage to reach the shore safely. You can wait for my return inside that dead oak tree. The one that has its branches hanging in the water. I'll leave you with these cautious words of advice. There is grave danger all around you. So no matter how tired or hungry you become, do not fall asleep until you reach the safety of the oak tree. Do not take gifts from smiling strangers. Stay on your guard at all times, and rely on your instincts, for they are your most trusted ally. If you become afraid, ask the Supreme Spirit for His protection, but above everything else, know your greatest strength is your belief in yourself. Farewell, Carlos, until we meet again."

As soon as Nathaniel flew away, Carlos started thinking about how he was going to get off the lily pad. He was pretty anxious too, as he was already starting to get hungry.

Just then he saw a huge pair of eyes staring at him from just below the surface of the pond. It made him feel creepy to be stared at so he hollered out, "Hey you down there, why are you staring at me?" The catfish came closer to the surface and said, "I'm staring at you because I've never seen a caterpillar out here in the middle of the pond and I'm wondering how you got here."

"A friend of mine, who's a knight, brought me here for a test. If I pass it, he's going to make me his squire when he returns."

"If he really was your friend, and a knight like you said, he wouldn't have left you out here all by yourself. Everybody knows that caterpillars can't swim. So tell me smarty pants, how do you plan on making it back to the shore?"

"I haven't quite figured that out yet, but I do know that Nathaniel is my friend because he has already saved my life. So there's nothing you or anybody else can say that will change my mind."

While Carlos was talking, the catfish was plotting on how he could trick him closer to the edge of the lily pad. Next to the grasshoppers and crickets, caterpillars were his favorite food. Besides knowing that caterpillars couldn't swim, he also knew they had ferocious appetites. "I bet you're hungry, aren't you? Tell you what, why don't I swim over to the shore and pick you a few juicy leaves to snack on."

"Oh that would be very kind of you," Carlos replied.

It took only a few minutes for the catfish to return. When Carlos saw him swim up to the lily pad with the leaves in his mouth, he became almost mad with hunger, and quickly crawled towards the awaiting feast. When he was just a few steps away, he suddenly remembered Nathaniel's words of caution, "Don't take any gifts from smiling strangers," and stopped dead in his tracks.

Carlos was lucky that he stopped when he did because if he would have taken another step, the catfish would have leaped up out of the water and swallowed him whole. Although Carlos was hungrier than he had ever been in his whole life, his instincts told him that this was one meal he would have to go without. Several minutes passed with the two of them just looking at each other and not moving a muscle. When the catfish realized that he wasn't going to trick Carlos any closer, he accepted his defeat with a grunt, and quickly swam away without saying another word.

"That was a pretty close call," Carlos thought, 'I'd better start paying more attention to what is going on around me, or I'll end up in someone's stomach." And he did just that for the rest of the day. He never imagined that there would so much activity on just a small pond. There were many different types of insects and birds flying this way and that, and he actually saw a spider walk on water. That was truly an amazing sight! There were big frogs and little frogs hopping and swimming about, and because the water was crystal clear and not too deep, he could see that besides catfish, the pond contained many other types of fish as well.

As the afternoon slowly passed, he also saw two orange and green turtles sunning themselves on a nearby log, and a blue-black water snake that was so long, it seemed to take forever to swim past him. On the banks of the pond, he saw a raccoon washing his food, and a cougar and coyote drinking.

When the sun went down and the moon came out, it started to rain heavily. Now, on top of being tired, lonely and very, very tired, he was getting soaking wet and colder by the minute. This had been the longest and most event filled day of his entire life, and even though he tried to be brave and not cry, when it started to thunder and lightening, he couldn't hold back his tears any longer.

It continued to rain on and off the rest of the night, but when the sun started to crest the horizon it stopped. Carlos had managed to stay awake the entire night. He did so by counting stars and singing every song that he knew. He even made up a few of his own. When the morning sun had warmed him, he once again started to think about how he was going to get off the lily pad. While he was thinking about this, he saw swimming in his direction the blue-black water snake that he had seen the previous day. When the snake got near, Carlos said, "Good morning Mr. Snake," in his friendliest voice. The snake stopped swimming and replied, "And good morning to you little fellow. May I ask you why you are out here in the middle of the pond all by yourself?"

"I am waiting for my friend to come back. What's your name and where are you going?"

"My name is Victor and I'm going hunting for my breakfast."

"What are you hunting for?"

"Mostly frogs, as they're the easiest to catch, but I also eat crawfish, lizards and mice when they come to the shoreline to drink."

"Do you eat caterpillars?"

"No, I don't," Victor said. "Water snakes do not eat insects."

"I'm really happy to hear that," Carlos said with a big smile on his face, "But how do I know you're telling the truth?"

"At this moment, there's no way for me to prove my word, but in defense of my own honor, I'll say this," I believe that to tell a lie is the absolute worst harm you can commit on your character; therefore, I would not lie to you because I would be lying to myself, and only fools lie to themselves."

Although Carlos could not explain why he believed Victor, his instincts told him that the water snake had a good heart and spoke the truth. So he asked him, "Would you mind giving me a ride over to that dead oak tree. I would be very grateful if you did."

"It would be a pleasure to carry you there, all you have to do is crawl on top of my head and we'll be on our way."

While they were swimming towards the shoreline, Carlos was amazed at how graceful Victor glided through the water. It was really quite beautiful to watch. When they arrived at the oak tree and Carlos had crawled onto it, he then turned to Victor and said, "I will be eternally in your debt. If there's anyway I can ever return your favor, please do not hesitate to call on me."

"I'll do just that little fellow," Victor said smilingly, and swam away.

As soon as the water snake left, Carlos raced up the oak tree and jumped onto a nearby raspberry bush. By the time the sun had reached its zenith, Carlos had stuffed his belly full of the delicious raspberry leaves. He then climbed back onto the oak tree and up its trunk. When he found an old woodpecker hole, he crawled into it and immediately fell into a deep sound sleep.

Chapter two: Where Ever Lies Your Heart, There Lies Your Treasure

When Carlos awoke the next morning and stuck his head out of the woodpecker hole, he saw Nathaniel sleeping on one of the oak branches. "He must have returned during the night. I'd better let him sleep for a while, as he's probably tired from all that flying he had to do." A few hours later, while Carlos was watching a couple of frisky squirrels chase each other up and down and round and round a nearby willow tree, he heard Nathaniel say, "Good morning Carlos and how is my new found friend?"

"And good morning to you Sir Knight, now that I know you've returned quite safely, I'm quite well."

"Thank you for your concern. The first thing you must tell me how you managed to get off that lily pad?"

Very proudly, Carlos old him every single detail of his adventure."

"That was a very brave thing you did, asking Victor to give you a ride to shore. Even I would have been afraid of that. But you said you weren't the least bit afraid of him. Would you please tell me why?"

"Victor made me realize that a person's word is their greatest treasure, and if you believe this with all your heart you will never tell a lie under any circumstances. You also told me to trust my instincts, and that is what I did."

"I believe you've learned one of life's most valuable lessons; therefore, I'm now going to tell you the rules of conduct which all knights must live by.

Since a knight is both a champion and servant of the Supreme Spirit's creatures, his conduct should always be honorable towards those he serves. Which means he must constantly strive to stay on the path of righteousness. A knight does this through right thought, right speech, right action and right living. For the rest of your life, you will make many decisions between right and wrong. Everyone does, but as long as you listen with your heart you will never wander from this noble path.

You should also know that a knight is a defender of the small, the weak and the helpless—even if he has to put his own life into harm's way. And finally, a knight is always: helpful to those in need, loyal to his friends, and truthful in matters entrusted to him. Did you understand everything I just said, Carlos."

"Yes, I did, Nathaniel."

"Then you are ready to pledge your allegiance to me and become my squire."

"Yes, I am."

Before I take your pledge I need first to say this: I swear to you that I will never forsake you for anything in the world. I will never ask you to do anything that I would not do myself, and I will always have your best interest at heart. Now then, I want you to repeat after me: I, Carlos Caterpillar, do solemnly swear to live an honorable life, and to be mindful to my mentor in all endeavors of knighthood."

As soon as Carlos had repeated the pledge, Nathaniel said' "Congratulations, you are now a knight's squire."

At that moment Carlos felt so proud that his chest was almost bursting with pride and happiness. It was hard to believe that he, just a mere caterpillar, had actually taken the first step toward becoming a Knight of the Forest. Wow! Just wait until his friends back in the garden hear about this! He made a promise to himself, that he would try his utmost to be the best squire the knighthood had ever known.

"I don't want to dampen your celebration Carlos, but duty calls us. Yesterday, while I was flying back here to meet you, I was told by a red tailed hawk that one of Queen Victoria's bees (a captain of her guard), was asking of my whereabouts. It must be something of vital importance because Queen Victoria has the largest bee hive in the forest, so we should go and try to find him."

It didn't take long to locate the Queen's captain because almost everyone knew Nathaniel, and when the word got out that he needed help to find a particular bee, the whole country side seemed to come alive to assist him.

Shortly thereafter, a flock of fast flying sparrows told them the bee they were looking for was in a meadow on the other side of Rebecca's house. Thanking them, Nathaniel told Carlos to hop on and they immediately flew there.

When they spotted the honey bee sitting on a dandelion, they landed next to him and Nathaniel said, "Greetings Captain, long time no see." Although they were close friends and had shared many adventures together, it had been several summers since thy had last seen each other.

"My heart soars like an eagle to see you again!" the captain said joyously. And who is this fine looking caterpillar with you, Nathaniel?"

"This is Carlos, and he's my squire. Carlos, this is Captain Blade. He's the captain of Queen Victoria's Royal Guard."

Bowing respectfully, Carlos said, "It is my honor to meet you sir."

"What brings you out of the forest, Captain Blade?"

"Queen Victoria has requested your immediate presence, Nathaniel."

"May I be so bold to ask why her majesty has requested my presence?"

"For the last eleven days Boris and his band of pirate wasps has been raiding the Queen's hive. They've murdered over a hundred of her workers, and I've lost nearly that many soldiers trying to defend the hive. They've also stolen over a gallon of honey from the royal pantry. If these raids continue, the Queen is doubtful that she'll be able to feed her hive through the winter. As you know, these wasps are fierce fighters and almost immune to our stingers, so we're in desperate need of your assistance."

"This is a very serious situation. We should probably leave right now as it will take us the rest of the day to reach the hive."

Just as soon as Carlos has crawled onto Nathaniel's back they took off.

Carlos was very impressed with how quickly Nathaniel had decided on what course of action to take. He now completely understood what true loyalty to your friends meant.

They flew upwards until they were high above the tree tops. When they reached the edge of the forest they were met by a full company of Captain Blade's soldier bees, who arranged themselves in a perfect V formation around the three of them, and onwards they flew. Whenever the wind shifted, the Captain issued a brisk command to his troops to change the level of flight a few degrees up or down, so they could better fly on the air currents, which were like waves above the forest.

For the entire day, without stopping to rest, they flew deeper and deeper into the forest. Carlos tried to stay awake, but the buzzing of the bee wings was making him drowsy. Just before he fell asleep, he thought how wonderful it was going to be, when he, too, would be able to fly like the birds and the bees.

When the sun started to dip below the horizon they landed at Queen Victoria's hive, which was in a huge hollowed out oak tree. When Carlos awoke, there were hundreds of bees buzzing and cheering all around them. He heard one of them say, "Look, it's Nathaniel, the Queen's favorite knight. She probably sent for him with the hope that he'll be able to stop Boris from raiding our hive."

They were led inside by one of the Queen's chamber maids, and told that her majesty had already retired for the evening; therefore, they would have an audience with her first thing in the morning. The chambermaid then took them to one of the royal apartments. When they got inside some other attendants brought them some freshly picked mint leaves, cool spring water and royal honey, which was sealed in acorn shells. Because he had never tasted honey before, this meal was by far the most delicious he had ever enjoyed.

After they were through eating, the Captain and Nathaniel got into a deep discussion on how to stop Boris and his band of thieving pirates.

"The way I see it, since we can't out fight him, we're going to either out think or out bluff them," Nathaniel said.

"And how, pray tell, do you propose we do that?" replied the Captain.

"What is the one insect wasps fear more than any other?"

"Why that would have to be a scorpion, but they live in the desert and are very savage and solitary creatures."

"That's true, but they are also very proud and honest and have a reputation for hating wasps, so maybe we can make a deal with one of them to come here and guard the entrance to the hive, and we'll pay him in honey. I'm also going to propose that her majesty allow me to go and have council with Boris tomorrow."

"All things considered, I don't think that's such a good idea. Boris is not only a cold blooded murderer, he's also a ruthless backstabber, and I wouldn't trust him further than I can spit! Besides, he wouldn't honor any treaty you made with him. The only thing that Boris understands is having his way, and violence," the Captain said almost shouting.

"I don't trust him one bit either, but hopefully he's smart enough to realize that in the end he can't defeat the combined forces of the knighthood; no one can! What I plan on doing, to avoid an all out war and to save as many lives as possible, is offer him a fair ultimatum; either he immediately stops his terrorist raids, disband his pirates and never return to the forest, or I'll ask the Council of Knights to hunt him down and destroy him. What say you to this, Captain Blade?"

"On second thought, I think they are both excellent ideas, Nathaniel. We'll propose them to the Queen in the morning."

With that agreed upon, they decided to bring the meeting to a close and retire for the night.

"As soon as Captain Blade left the apartment, Carlos said "Nathaniel, may I ask you a question?"

"You can ask me anything, but that doesn't mean I'll have an answer."

"Would you please tell me the difference between killing and murder?"

"For someone so young, that's a very serious and complex question to ask, but since it involves one of the laws of nature the Supreme Spirit has given us to live by, I'll do my best to explain the difference. When an animal takes a life of another to feed itself and its children, this is a righteous kill according to the laws of nature, but if you take the life of any living being because of greed, anger, hatred, pride, jealousy or sport, this would be murder. Humans, who are supposed to be the most intelligent and the Supreme Spirit's greatest creation, are by the worst offenders of this law. Since the dawning of time they have committed countless murders, not just to their own kind, but to almost every other species on the planet without the slightest remorse. They're the only ones who murder for the sheer pleasure of it, which they call sport, then proudly mount the heads, horns and carcasses of the animals they've murdered on the wall of their dwellings and call them trophies. You should bear in memory that they also like to collect insects, especially butterflies! When you transform into one, if you ever see a human wandering the country side with a cone shaped net, it's highly advisable that you immediately turn around and fly in the opposite direction.

"Where Boris is concerned, you should by now clearly understand why he's a thief and a murderer, and why he and his band of pirates must be forever band from entering the forest again."

"Since we're going to have a very busy day tomorrow, and I'm very tired, it's best we conclude this conversation and go to sleep, so I'll beseech your leave and bid you a good night."

Although Carlos was still wide awake, and had many other questions running through his mind, he honored his knight's request by saying, "And good night to you Nathaniel, may you rest peacefully."

One of the questions Carlos wanted to ask Nathaniel was if he would allow him to go when he had council with Boris. Because of the obvious dangers involved, he didn't foresee his knight allowing him to, so he decided to think up a few good reasons to persuade him. While he was thinking about what to say, and all the wondrous things he had discovered about life since meeting Nathaniel, he fell asleep, and had a marvelous dream about flying solo high above the clouds where only eagles dared to go.

Early the next morning when Carlos woke up, Captain Blade had returned, and he and Nathaniel were eating their breakfast together. "Good morning Carlos," Nathaniel said, "Come and join us, but you must hurry as we'll soon be having an audience with the Queen." A short while later, one of the Queen's attendants appeared in the doorway of their apartment and said, "The Queen bids your presence Sir Knight, and yours too, Captain Blade. If you'll be so kind as to follow me we'll proceed to her chambers.

While they were walking toward the Queen's chambers, which was deep in the center of the hive, Nathaniel said, "Carlos, since I know you've never been to court, allow me to instruct you on the proper way to conduct yourself while you're in the Queen's presence. After we've been announced, bow respectfully and then remain silent unless she asks you a direct question. Bear in memory that besides being the ruler of the hive, she's also the ruler of the entire forest."

"That means she's the absolute boss, so mind your manners and your curious tongue young lad", Captain Blade added.

When they passed through the entrance to the Queen's chambers, which was guarded by several tough looking soldier bees, another attendant said in a loud clear voice, "Your majesty, I present the Knight Nathaniel, his Squire Carlos and Captain Blade."

After being announced, they bowed to the Queen and she said, "Come forth, Nathaniel."

"Always obedient to thy Graces will, I've come to know your pleasure? Nathaniel said in a dignified voice.

"I've summoned you to court because I believe your courage, honor and intelligence qualifies you best, to remedy a life and death situation that has plagued my hive. I'm sure that Captain Blade has informed you that my hive has been placed in dire straits by the raids of Boris and his band of pirates. My royal counters have informed me that my honey stores are at an all time low, and even though my workers have been working overtime to replenish the lost, they're not sure that I'll have enough to feed my hive through the winter months. If my hive were to perish due to starvation, my bees wouldn't be able to pollinate the flowers, fruit trees and other plants when they blossom in the spring. Therefore these raids must be immediately be stopped, or they'll wreak havoc on the entire forest. Have you and Captain Blade thought up a plan to halt these raids, Sir Knight?"

"I believe we have, your Majesty. Within the hour, because time is of the essence, you need to send a special envoy into the desert to procure the services of a scorpion here and guard the entrance to the hive. As long as you have a scorpion standing sentry there, no wasp would dare to enter, as they are deadly afraid of them. We can arrange his transportation here with one of our feathered knights, and his commission can be paid in honey. Although the scorpion would prevent the raids from reoccurring here, it doesn't solve the problem. Boris is clever enough to simply switch his raids onto other hives. This is the main reason that I should go and have council with him. I believe that I can persuade him to stop his terrorist raids and disband his pirates under the threat of the Council of Knights hunting him down and destroying him."

"Do you agree that this is the best way to deal with the situation Captain Blade?"

"Yes, I do, majesty."

"I hereby grant permission to do what ever you think is necessary, that's in the best interest of the hive. When will you be leaving Sir Knight, and who will be going with you?"

"I'll be leaving when the sun sets your majesty and no one will be accompanying me, as I think it's best that I go alone."

"Then go in peace, Nathaniel, and may the Supreme Spirit watch over and protect you."

When Carlos heard Nathaniel say that he would go alone, he was very disappointed as he had his heart totally set on going. Maybe he would still change his mind before he left.

Chapter Three: You Never Know The Strength Of Anything Until It's Been Tested.

On the way back to their apartment, Nathaniel said to Carlos, "While I'm gone I'll leave you with a close friend of mine who's a monk and spiritual advisor to the Queen. Although he was blinded in a forest fire three summers ago, he's very wise. Before he became a monk he was a knight. You should also know that I was his squire before I became a knight."

"What's a monk, Nathaniel?"

"A monk is someone who has given up all his worldly pursuits and devoted his life to spiritual enlightenment."

Leaving the hive they only had to fly a short distance, where upon they flew into a dark, damp cave that was on the side of a steep hill above a fast flowing stream.

After landing inside the cave, Nathaniel pointed to the ceiling and said, "I'd like you to meet my dear friend and mentor Christopher."

Carlos looked up and there hanging upside down was a rust colored animal that had the head of a fox (which was badly burned) and hairless wings which he had wrapped around his body.

"Greetings, Nathaniel, you honor my dwelling with your presence. How have you been treating life since we last saw each other?"

"As you taught me Your Grace, I cherish each day as if it's the only one I got."

"As long as you continue to do so, each day will be a life time unto itself." Who have you brought with you, Nathaniel?"

"I've brought you my squire to meet you. His name is Carlos and he's a Monarch caterpillar from the border town of Del Rio."

"He must be a very special caterpillar as you have never taken a squire before." "That's true, your Grace, I did so because being a quick learner, he's brave and has a quality of heart, character and spirit that's very rare in someone his age. Furthermore, I believe he'll make a fine and brave knight one day. With your permission, what I'd like to do is leave him with you for a short while, as I have an urgent mission that demands my full attention."

"Of course he can stay with me. And for however long that's necessary. When will you be leaving, Nathaniel?"

"I'll leave when the moon is high. Between now and then there are several matters of grave importance that I must finalize with Captain Blade. I'll return tonight before I depart." With that said, Nathaniel turned around and flew out of the cave.

"Why don't you crawl up here next to me so that we can better get acquainted with each other."

After Carlos had crawled up the side of the cave and sat down beside him on a nearby ledge, Christopher said, "Would you like to hear a story that I once told Nathaniel when he was your age?"

"I'd love to", Carlos eagerly replied.

"One day a hawk swooped down and caught a young dove in her talons. As she flew back into the sky, the dove began to cry. He chastised himself for wandering away from where his parents had told him to stay—'If only I has listened to my parents, I wouldn't be in this predicament.'

"The hawk asked, "And where did your parents tell you to stay, you runt?" The dove answered, 'In the newly ploughed corn field."

"To the dove's surprise the hawk said, 'I can catch any dove I want any time I want. I will return you to the field and offer you one more hour of life. I will be looking for you, and in just an hour I will catch you, break your little neck, and eat you at once.' And the hawk swooped down again and released the dove in the newly plowed corn field.

"Surprisingly, the young dove immediately climbed up on a mound of earth, and began to taunt the hawk.

"Angered, the hawk tucked her wings close to her sides and shot down at full speed, but the dove quickly ducked for cover in the furrow beneath the mound of earth, and the hawk missed the dove and landed with such force that she broke her breastbone and was killed instantly.

"While the dove was laughing and strutting around for making the hawk crash into the ground, a gray fox, who was nearly, heard him laughing and raced out of his burrow and ended the dove's life in one swift bite.

"What did you learn form this story, Carlos?"

"That you always listen to the advice of your parents and never gloat over someone's misfortune."

"Your answer tells me you are a very keen listener and I'm impressed with your insight; however, there is much more to learn from this story than meets the eye. The reason that both the dove and the hawk lost their lives was because they fell victim to their lower emotions. Which are: anger, hate, greed and pride. Your high emotions, which should always control your lower emotions, are: love, compassion, modesty and kindness. The reason that the hawk lost her life is because when she became angry she lost focus of her objective. This means that when you become angry your level of awareness lessens. The same principle applies to the dove. When you become too prideful and arrogant, your level of awareness drops."

"This is the main reason that we should practice being more mindful of our actions every day of our lives, Carlos."

"What can I do to become more mindful of my actions, your Grace?"

"You can start by becoming more aware of everything that you say and everything you do. You should also bear in memory the law of karma, which is 'what goes around comes around'.

"I'm not sure I completely understood that last part about karma, your Grace."

"That's okay, I didn't understand it the first time it was explained to me either. I'll explain what karma is in this manner. As long as we treat others kindly, we will be treated kindly in return, but if we treat others cruelly, sooner or later, we will suffer the same fate. Let's take what Boris and his band of pirates have done for example. They've broken just all the laws of nature the Supreme Spirit has given us to live an honorable life by; therefore, he and his comrades must now suffer the effects of their negative actions."

For the rest of the day, Carlos listened in wonderment to the bountiful wisdom of Christopher. Toward evening, Carlos said, "I have a bit of a quandary, your Grace, and I'd appreciate your advice."

"Speak freely, Squire."

"As you are aware, Nathaniel will be leaving when the moon is high to seek council with Boris. He told Captain Blade that he will be going alone. I understand this will probably a most dangerous mission, but if I'm to learn how to contend with the pitfalls, stumbling blocks and challenges of life, I should be at the side of my knight."

"Your words are strong and they have merit; however, since you became a knight's squire, the well-being of your life is in his hands. So whatever decision he makes in your behalf you should respect, as he has only your best interest at heart."

"Thank you for sharing those meaningful words of wisdom with me, your Grace."

"It was my pleasure to do so. I must leave you now as it's time for me to go out for my nightly feeding. You'll be safe here until Nathaniel returns. Please give him my regards and tell him that I said, 'you'll never know the strength of anything until it's been tested. Peace with you, Carlos."

After Christopher flew out of the cave, Carlos, who besides being always hungry and always curious too, started wondering what the monk's message to Nathaniel meant. He also wondered how a blind bat managed to fly without crashing into the walls of the cave.

He didn't have to wait very long because soon thereafter he heard Nathaniel flying toward him. When he landed next to Carlos he said, "It does my heart well to see you, Carlos. How was your visit with Christopher?"

"It was absolutely wonderful, Sir Knight! I learned many new things from him."

"I am to hear what you did. Would you be so kind as to share some of your new found wisdom with me?"

"I learned that good qualities are things you should embrace and cultivate, for they are amply rewarded and that vices were bad things that should be avoided at all cost, for they bring nothing but trouble and punishment."

"I also learned that doing good deeds advances your life and leads to a greater and fuller development of self and that bad deeds accomplish the contrary."

"Since the day that I met you, Carlos, I've been greatly impressed with your intelligence, insight and how quickly you learn things. I believe the Supreme Spirit has truly blessed you with special qualities because although you're still a child, you have the understanding of an adult."

"Thank you, Sir Knight, for a beautiful compliment. Does this mean that you'll consider allowing me to go with you when you seek council with Boris?"

"I'll consider it, if you promise that you'll do exactly as I tell you to do without question."

"I promise that I will. By the way, Christopher told me to tell you that you 'never know the strength of anything until it's tested,"

"Do you know why he sent that message to me, Carlos?"

"No, sir, I don't."

"You must have made quite an impression on him, which is not easy, I assure you. Because of this, he told me that I should consider allowing you to go, so that is what I'm going to do."

"Now then, before we depart I want you to listen closely to what I'm about to say because our lives may depend on how well you follow my instructions. In just a little while we'll be flying into the swamp, which is about ten miles from here. There's a small island in the middle of it that's called Dragon's Pit. This is where Boris and his band of pirates have made their lair. As soon as we land I want you to quickly hide yourself. It will be your duty to watch my back while I'm having council with Boris. Under no circumstances are you to reveal yourself because it would only take one wasp sting to kill you. Once we land on Dragon's Pit Island, it won't take long for Boris to know we're there because he has spies everywhere."

"The last thing we should do before we depart is to say a prayer, and ask the Supreme Spirit to protect us while we're on our mission. Bowing their heads, Nathaniel said' "Oh Great Spirit, my squire and I beseech your protection from the evilness we are about to encounter. We ask you to be our guardian and to shield us from the forces of our enemies."

When they flew out of the monk's cave, there was a full moon shining brightly in the night sky. Flying swiftly above the tree tops, they headed due south towards the swamp and the fate which waited for them there.

Because dragon flies were the fastest flying insects in the world, it only took them about a half hour to travel the distance to the swamp. While they were flying over it and heading toward Dragon's Pit Island, Carlos was thinking that he had never seen such a spooky, eerie place before, not even in his worst nightmare.

When they landed on the beach of the island, Carlos quickly crawled off Nathaniel's back as fast as he could and hid himself in a nearby hollowed out log that had washed up on the beach. From inside the log, Carlos could see several fire flies blinking on and off above Nathaniel's head. One of them rushed off quickly across the water, and Carlos thought, "He's probably going to warn Boris that we are here."

It seemed like only a few minutes had gone by when suddenly Carlos saw eight mean looking yellow and black wasps landing around Nathaniel. One of them, who was a bit larger and the meanest looking of the bunch, boldly stepped forward and said, "Nathaniel, you're either crazy or a fool to come to my island alone, or maybe you have a death wish."

"No, Boris, it's not I who has taken leave of the senses, as evident by the bloody havoc you and your pirates have waged against the peace and livelihood of the whole forest. It is for these crimes that I have been sent by Queen Victoria to offer you a proposition. Either you immediately halt your terrorist raids, return the royal honey that you have stolen and disband your pirates, or she'll declare you an outlaw and prohibit you and your comrades from ever entering the forest again. What say you to her proposition, Boris?"

"She's got a lot of nerve offering me such a weak and one sided proposition, especially when there's absolutely nothing she can do to stop me from doing what ever I want!"

"Oh, but she does, Boris. She has the command of the Council of Knights to enforce her rule, and if they come after you they'll hunt you down and your whole band without mercy. So use your smarts, Boris, You've got to know in the long run you can't win against the combined forces of the knighthood, so quit now while you're ahead and still alive."

After Nathaniel had said this, Boris took a few steps back and made a motion to the other wasps to gather around him. Although Carlos could not hear what they were talking about from inside the log, he could tell they were having a heated argument by the angry expressions on their faces. Suddenly, they broke from their huddle and attacked Nathaniel without warning, stinging him repeatedly. Nathaniel fought back gallantly, but in the blink of an eye the attack was over and the wasps flew off laughing at their treachery, leaving Nathaniel severely wounded.

Carlos was in a state of shock, having witnessed his best friend's attack. When he crawled out of the log and over to where Nathaniel was laying, he saw many stingers sticking out of the brave knight's body. He cried out, "Nathaniel, what can I do to help you?" In a very moanful voice because he was in much pain, Nathaniel said, "Carlos, because of the poison, that's in the wasp stingers I will soon loose consciousness and go into a coma. You must find a healer and bring him to me if I'm to be saved. My life is in your hands."

Right after he said this he passed out. At first, Carlos thought he had died and almost panicked, but then he realized that his knight was still breathing, although it was weak and shallow.

"Now what am I supposed to do? Here I am in the middle of a bloody swamp and I've got to find a healer." Looking around, Carlos realized that except for a few young fire flies playing catch me out over the water he was entirely alone. While he sat there wondering what to do, it appeared, to his dismay that the water was slowly creeping towards them. He didn't know that the full moon made the tide rise faster than normal. It was at that moment that he got a splendid idea.

Calling out to the fire flies, he said, "Hey you guys come over here for a moment I want to talk to you." When the seven fire flies flew over, Carlos said to them, "How would you guys like to earn some royal honey?" One of them, who looked to be the oldest, replied, "What would we have to do?"

"All you would have to do is fly to Queen Victoria's hive and tell them that Nathaniel has been severely injured and needs a healer right away and they'll reward you with all the honey that you can eat."

"If we help you and Boris finds out he'll kill us!"

"I don't think you have to worry about that too much, as late as it is he has probably already gone to sleep; besides, who said that you have to come back to this creepy swamp and live in fear of Boris all the time."

'The caterpillar is right you guys; we don't ever have to come back here; we can go anywhere we want to", replied the same fire fly. "Lets take a vote on it, who's in favor of helping the caterpillar and never coming back here?" At the same time they all shouted,

"I am."

"Okay then, we might as well leave right now and fly directly to the Queen's hive. See you later caterpillar." With that said they immediately flew off toward the forest.

Chapter Four: At The Moment Of Choice I Will Exercise Integrity

While Carlos was talking to the fire flies the water had almost crept up to where Nathaniel was laying. He knew that it would take at least an hour for anyone to return from the hive, so he had to move Nathaniel to higher ground or he would drown. Gripping Nathaniel's front leg in his mouth, Carlos started dragging him back off the beach. It took all of his strength because Nathaniel weighed three times what he did, but with great effort he finally managed to pull him into the tall swamp grass.

Moving Nathaniel was the hardest ask he ever had to perform in his entire life and it had almost exhausted him; still, he felt proud that he was able to accomplish it. He hoped with all his might that a healer would return soon because it appeared that that Nathaniel's condition was getting much worse, as he now had a high fever and his body had begun to swell.

Looking out over the murky swamp water he thought he heard a buzzing off in the distance. Wanting to get a better view he quickly crawled up one of the stems of tall swamp grass. When he reached the top he saw to his immediate delight Captain Blade, Christopher and a dragon fly who had the same color markings as Nathaniel flying in his direction, and being lead by one of the young fire flies he had talked to earlier. As loud as he could shout he started calling to them, "Over here, captain, we're over here!"

After they had all landed, except the fire fly who flew back across the water, Christopher said, "Carlos, this is Michael, and he's the most renowned dragonfly healer in the forest."

"Greetings, Squire Carlos, if we're going to save your knight we must act swiftly.

I've brought some special healing herbs with me that we have to place on all of Nathaniel's wounds. These herbs will counteract the poison that's in the wasp stingers. Carlos can help me apply these herbs. While we're doing this the captain and Christopher can go down to the water's edge and bring back enough mud to cover all of Nathaniel's wounds."

Working together as a team it only took the four of them a short while to doctor Nathaniel. When they were finished, Michael said,

"We've done everything that we can for him; his fate is now in the hands of the Supreme Spirit. We'll know by morning if he'll recover or not."

"Since we're no longer needed here, Christopher and myself will return to the forest. Queen Victoria has called an emergency meeting of the Council of Knights to promptly deal with Boris and we should be there to offer our aid to them. Before we depart I want to congratulate you Carlos on your loyalty to your knight. Your quick thinking and courage probably saved his life. In the spring, when you become a butterfly and go before the Council to be voted into knighthood, it will be my pleasure to speak in your behalf," said the captain.

"It will be my honor to also speak in your behalf", Christopher said. We'll return tomorrow to see how Nathaniel is doing."

After Christopher said this, he and the captain bid farewell to Carlos and Michael; then flew off toward the forest. Right after they left, the always curious Carlos said, "Michael, why did you become a healer."

"I became a healer for several reasons. One of them was because my father was a healer and his father before him, so it's been a tradition in my family for several generations, but that's not the main reason I became one. I became a healer because I know the Great Spirit smiles on us whenever we help someone, no matter how small the courtesy. Carlos, Christopher told me that you have a thirst for knowledge; therefore, I'm going to share with you the greatest advice my father ever gave to me. He said, 'At the moment of choice we should exercise integrity.' Do you understand what that means, Carlos?"

"No, sir, I don't."

"We know that exercise means to do something, and integrity is the root for our character; therefore, every time we have to make a choice—which is something we have to do many times a day—we should always try our utmost to do what's right. In other words, as long as we listen to our hearts we'll never go wrong. I've had a very busy day and I'm very tired, Carlos, but one of us needs to stay awake to watch over Nathaniel. Do you think you'll be able to do this until morning?"

"Yes, sir, I do."

"Very well then, if his condition gets any worse do not hesitate to wake me. Good night, Carlos."

It appeared that as soon as Michael shut his eyes he fell asleep, leaving Carlos alone with his thoughts. Looking over Nathaniel, who seemed to be on the brink of death, he questioned his own future because he had no idea what he would do if his knight didn't recover. Could he find another knight willing to take him as his squire? Thinking about all this made him terribly sad. Wondering how he could help matters, he remembered what Nathaniel had told him when he left him on the lily pad, the day they had met. Carlos looked up at the heavens and from the bottom of his heart he prayed, "Oh Great Spirit, hear my voice. Before you, in grave sickness lies your obedient servant, Nathaniel, a true and brave Knight of the Forest, who risked his life defending your laws of nature. If ever there was a life deserving your blessings, it is his. He is my best friend and I could not ask for a better one. If a life must be taken this night, take mine instead, which I offer without reservations."

Right after Carlos said these words, it appeared that one of the stars started to grow brighter and move towards him. Brighter and brighter it grew and closer and close it came. To his wide eyed astonishment the ball of luminous light descended upon Nathaniel and totally engulfed him. Then a beautiful voice came from it, saying, "Do not fear what you see, Carlos, for I am Finn, the Spirit of the Forest. I have come to heal Nathaniel because his honorable dedication to the knighthood and the faith we have entrusted him with, is worthy our favor. Carlos, know that our spirit is in every living creature, every drop of water, every blade of grass and in every grain of sand in the universe. Nothing can have life without our presence. Wherever you go and whatever you do, our love will be there with you. Before I depart I want you always to bear this foremost in memory: your life will only be what you make of it, no more, no less. Peace be with you, Carlos, let what you have witnessed here this night remain with you only."

As quickly as the ball of luminous light had descended from the heavens, it rose back up until it disappeared as just another star in the night sky, leaving Carlos to wonder if he had dreamt the whole event.

A few hours later the morning sun started to rise on the eastern horizon, and Michael awakened.

"Good morning, Carlos, how is our patient doing?"

"He's doing just fine", Carlos replied with a big smile on his face, thinking, "If only he knew what happened while he slept."

Up until that moment, Carlos hadn't realized how extremely tired he was. Crawling deeper into the swamp grass, he curled himself into a small ball and immediately fell into a deep, sound sleep.

Later that afternoon when Carlos was awakened, to his joyous surprise he heard Michael and Nathaniel talking. Running over to where they were, his heart was so filled with delight that his knight had recovered, that he started jumping up and down with happiness, shouting to him, "Nathaniel, Nathaniel, I'm so glad to see that you're well!"

"I'm not completely cured just yet, Carlos. I'm still very weak and I get dizzy when I try to fly, but Michael has assured me that I'll be okay in about three days. You must tell me everything that happened after I lost consciousness."

After Carlos told him, except the part about Finn's visit, Nathaniel said, "Because you risked your life to save mine and stood by my side when I was not able to help myself, you've proven your loyalty and friendship and I will be eternally grateful and in your debt. In the spring when you become a butterfly, it will be my great honor to recommend you to the Council for the acceptance into the knighthood.

Chapter Five: It Doesn't Matter What You Say, It Only Matters What You Do.

For the rest of the summer Nathaniel and Carlos had many adventures together and traveled far and wide throughout the Queen's domain. Boris and his band of pirates were driven from the forest by the knighthood and never heard of again. When he wasn't traveling with Nathaniel, he would visit Christopher so he could learn from his vast store of knowledge.

In the fall when the leaves started to change colors and the wind blew colder, Carlos knew that the time had finally come for him to perform one of the greatest miracles in nature. With Nathaniel's help they found a safe place high in the branches of a pecan tree which was near Christopher's cave. There Carlos spun a turquoise colored cocoon and sealed himself within it. He then fell onto the deepest sleep of his life.

Three months later, in early spring, Carlos emerged from his cocoon. His beautiful wings were still wet and wrinkled so he had to flex them for a few minutes to get the blood circulating. When they were dry and fully spread in their colorful splendor, he took off with a shout of glee! He quickly discovered that flying was the greatest sensation he had ever experienced. He flew high and low, he did figure eights and loops-de-loops, and because flying was so much fun he flew the entire morning without stopping to rest. When he did start to grow tired he landed on the nearest flower, which was a Blue Bonnet and stuck his long thin tongue into its center and drank the sweet nectar from it. While he was drinking, a bit of the pollen that was in the flower got onto his hind legs. When he flew to the next flower he transferred this pollen onto it, so like the honey bees he helped pollinate the flowers and the fruit trees throughout the forest.

After he had drunk his fill and rested a while, he decided it was time to locate Nathaniel. Knowing that he was close to Christopher's cave he immediately flew there. Flying into the monk's dwelling he saw him hanging from his usual roost. Although he looked like he was sleeping because his eyes were shut, to Carlos' surprise when he got near him, Christopher said, "Who has come to visit me? If you come in peace you'll be received in peace."

"It is Carlos, your Grace, Nathaniel's squire, I've come seeking the whereabouts of my knight."

"It is your good fortune that you have come this day because Nathaniel was here just this morning. He is now with the Council of Knights and I'm expecting him to return this afternoon. Will I have the pleasure of your company till he returns?"

"Yes, your Grace, I would enjoy a visit with you very much, thank you for asking."

"Carlos, Nathaniel told me that he's going to recommend you for acceptance into the knighthood to-day, and because you deserve our favor I'm going to second his nomination. Are you prepared to go in front of the Council to be interviewed?"

"I think so", Carlos said nervously. "What will take place when I do?"

"There are seven members on the Council and they were all elected by the knighthood. After Nathaniel recommends you they'll ask you to explain why you want to become a knight. Then they'll take a vote on your acceptance. You must receive a majority vote for admission. Do you think you are ready for this? Yes, sir, I believe that I am."

"After this you'll have an audience with the Queen where you pledge your allegiance to her. Then she'll knight you."

Carlos heard a familiar buzzing enter the cave, where upon he saw Nathaniel flying toward him. After landing he said, "My heart soars like an eagle to see you again, Carlos, you have certainly turned into a beautiful butterfly."

"Thank you", Carlos said blushing.

"Are you ready to go in front of the Council of Knights?"

"Yes, sir, I believe I am."

"Then we should probably leave right now as they're expecting me to return within the hour."

The three of them flew to a circular clearing behind the Queen's hive where the council of seven knights had gathered. The knights, who sat on rocks, which were also in a circle were: a peregrine falcon, who was the most majestic bird Carlos had ever seen, a bushy tailed fox, a mint green colored praying mantis, a tarantula with eight red eyes, an otter with beautiful light brown fur, a black and silver osprey, and sitting at the head of the council was a snow white eagle owl. It was she who spoke first. "Nathaniel, is this your squire Carlos the Monarch butterfly you would like to recommend to the knighthood?"

"Yes, madam, it is."

"He's awfully young to be a knight don't you think?", the eagle owl said.

"It is true that he's young, but I would stake my life on him being just as qualified as any of you. Actually, Carlos has the purest soul of any creature I've ever encountered.

Not only has he been totally loyal to me throughout his training, I've never known him to neglect his duties, tell a lie or break his word. If he tells you he's going to do something you can be assured it will be done. Furthermore, he was quick to help the sick and the handicapped, and did not hesitate to share food even when he was hungry. Best of all, I consider it an honor to have him as my friend."

"I too fully support his candidacy and would like to second his nomination", Christopher said.

Very well then, come into the Circle of Truth and tell us why you're worthy enough to be a knight", the eagle owl said. She then leaned over and whispered to the otter sitting next to her, "Carlos must be a really special squire to have two knights recommend him." Flying into the Circle of Truth, Carlos bowed respectfully to the council, then in a clear confident voice he said, "Thank you for those kind words of praise Nathaniel, I also consider your friendship an honor. One of the first commends my knight ever made to me was, 'It doesn't matter what you say; it only matters what you do.' The reason that I totally believe in that principle is because he and the other knights that I had contact with are a living testament of this wisdom. That's to say they just don't talk about what needs to be done. They do it every day. This more than anything else has made the greatest impression on my life. I mention this because I could give you a thousand and one reasons why I want to become a knight, but the reasons themselves are meaningless because words without action behind them are worthless. Since I became a Knight's squire, I've learned that it doesn't matter who you are, or if you're old or young, rich or poor, there's only two paths to travel. One is the path of light. The other is the path of darkness. If you choose the path of darkness, as the one Boris chose, in the end you'll have to suffer the dire consequences.

If you choose the path of life you'll be richly rewarded because good always triumphs over evil. I've chosen to travel the path of light because it makes my heart feel good to be helpful and to do good deeds to others; besides, I too know that it's the path that leads to heaven. It is for this reason, more than any other, that I want to become a Knight of the Forest. Thank you for hearing my plea."

When Carlos was through with his presentation he flew out of the Circle of Truth and landed next to Nathaniel and Christopher. The owl then said, "We'll now take a vote. All in favor of admitting Carlos into the knighthood say yes." In one voice the entire council of seven knights agreed upon his acceptance.

Smiling with much pride, Nathaniel said, "Allow me to be the first to congratulate you Carlos, you are the youngest knight ever to be accepted in the knighthood."

"Tell us how you feel", Christopher said.

"Since it's a dream come true, words alone can't express my joy and happiness", Carlos replied.

"Officially, you're not a knight until Queen Victoria knights you. We'll proceed to her chambers now for that to take place."

When they arrived at the queen's hive they were taken directly to her chambers. Upon entrance they were announced by the speaker-of-the-hive. "Your majesty, I present the Knight Nathaniel and the Knight-elect Carlos."

After they bowed to her, the queen said, "Greetings, Nathaniel, It's been brought to my attention that the Council recommended your squire for the knighthood."

"That's correct, Your Majesty."

"Then he should come forth to be recognized."

Stepping forward, Carlos knelt in front of his queen. She then said, "It's always one of the greatest pleasures to ordain a new knight, especially one that I have heard such marvelous things about. Carlos, do you swear to protect the lives of my subjects and defend the laws of nature?"

"I do swear, Your Majesty."

Then arise, Sir Carlos. From this day you are a Knight of the Forest."

When Carlos stood up, he was so excited that it felt like his head was in the clouds. This was by far the happiest day in his life. While he and Nathaniel were walking out of the queen's chambers—amidst the cheers and applause of her subjects, he remembered something that Christopher said about not wishing too hard for dreams to come true. He couldn't have meant all dreams. It seemed to Carlos that wishing for something good to come true, such as him becoming a Knight of the Forest, benefited the whole world; therefore, Christopher had to mean that you have to be very careful about wishing for something to come true that wasn't good.

After they got outside the hive and flew off, Nathaniel said, "Carlos, now that you're a knight, what do you plan on doing."

"First of all, I'm going to fly back to the garden that I was born in to visit my friends. I haven't seen some of them since I was a caterpillar. Then I'm going to take a little vacation south of the border. I heard that every year millions of Monarch Butterflies from all over the United States and Canada migrate to a particular valley in Mexico. Being with so many of my own kind would be truly an event of a life time. What are you going to do Nathaniel?"

"Christopher and I are flying to Lake Victoria this afternoon to help a swan to locate two of her missing chicks."

"It appears that we won't be seeing each other for a while", Carlos said sadly.

"That's true, but your friendship will always be right here with me", Nathaniel said pointing to his heart. "Before we depart from each other's company, I want you to learn this and learn it well: honor, charity and truth is your shield against the evil forces of this world. The more good that you do the stronger your shield becomes. Peace be with you my brother until we meet again." With that said, Nathaniel flew off toward Christopher's cave, and Carlos set off on his journey to Rebecca's garden.

Because he flew at a leisurely pace and stopped along the way to talk to almost everyone he met, it took him almost two days to reach the pond behind Rebekka's house. Circling it he asked the insects and animals who lived around the pond if they knew Victor, but no one had seen him that day. When he was just about ready to give up his search he saw a ripple in the water. Flying to it he was happy to see Victor swimming towards the shore. He called out to him, "Hey Victor look up here! It's me Carlos, and I've come back to visit you." When Victor looked up he didn't see Carlos the caterpillar, he saw an orange and black Monarch butterfly hovering in the air just above his head.

"It really makes my day brighter to see you again Carlos. What do I owe the pleasure of your visit?"

"I wanted to share my good fortune by letting you know that I am now a Knight of the Forest, and ask you if there was any way I could return the favor for helping me off that lily pad."

"As a matter of fact, there is. Lately, I've been feeling kind of lonely. I think it's time that I found a mate and started a family, but I'm the only water snake living on this pond. Do you know where I could find a wife?"

"If you were to follow the stream that the pond empties into, it flows all the way to Lake Victoria. It will take you three or four days of difficult swimming to get there, but I know there are many female water snakes living on the lake, so it will be easy for someone as handsome as you to find a pretty wife."

"Thank you for that information. I'll get started on my trip right away. Where are you flying to, Carlos?"

"I'm going to visit my childhood friends over in Rebecca's garden."

"Well, I hope you have a good visit with them."

"And I hope you find a pretty wife. The next time I'm near Lake Victoria I'll look you up. Until then, take care of yourself, Victor"

"You do the same Carlos."

Leaving the pond, Carlos flew across the meadow and entered the garden from the rear. Flying over the back fence a very frightening sight was revealed to him. Standing on her back porch, Rebecca was pointing her double barrel shotgun at Paco, the raven, who was busily digging up and eating the freshly planted seeds. With a burst of lightning speed he crossed the garden and flew in between Rebecca's gun and Paco. When she tried to take a different aim on him, Carlos continued to flutter right in front of her gun barrel no matter where she pointed it.

"Get out of the way you little stupid butterfly! I'm tired of that pesky black crow raiding my garden! I'm going to take care of him once and for all!"

When Paco heard Rebecca shouting, he turned around and saw Carlos fluttering in front of her gun—which prevented her from aiming at him. This greatly surprised him because he realized in just a split second that the butterfly was actually risking his own life to save his. This so shocked him he didn't know if he should try and take flight, or shut his eyes and take his last breath.

When Rebecca realized that the butterfly wasn't going to let her take aim, she let out a sigh of frustration and set her shot gun down and went back into the house, shaking her head in confusion to what she just witnessed.

As soon as Rebecca's screen door slammed shut, Paco flew up besides Carlos and said, "You're either the craziest or the bravest butterfly in the world to have risked your life in such a way, but I must thank you for saving my life."

"Your gratitude humbles my heart, but you need not thank me, for I am a Knight of the Forest, and it is my sworn duty to protect all living beings and defend the laws of nature."

On The For Real Side

Script for DVD "Change Instead of Chains"

By David Anglin/Bullis

What I'm about to tell you could change your life, enhance the quality of it, but you are going to have to listen closely, very closely with an open mind for this to happen. From the jump, it is important that you thoroughly understand, what I mean by asking you to listen to me with an open mind.

For a lot of people, depending on how much they want to change and/or improve the quality of their life, listening to someone with an open mind can be a lot more difficult than it appears. That is because you are going to have to put your personal biases (your likes and dislikes) on hold and not be judgmental while I am speaking to you. In other words, hear me all the way out before you start throwing stones at me.

So that we all can be on the same page, I should first tell you a little about my background. I am a career criminal; consequently, I have been in and out of prison my whole life.

My nightmare with the justice system began in 1965, when I entered adult prison at the age of sixteen, because I lied about my age, not wanting to be returned to Juvenile Hall where I had escaped from. I have since served over thirty-three years in three different states and one foreign country for charges of: armed robbery, breaking & entering, carrying a concealed weapon (two counts), murder, sexual assault, manslaughter, pandering and espionage.

I was a confirmed pothead for over twenty years and a hardcore cocaine addict for five. While I was an addict I committed crimes on a daily basis to support my habit and was never arrested for these.

Let me emphasize that I am not telling you any of this to boast about my past behavior in any sort of way. Actually, I am terribly ashamed of all the pain and havoc I have wrecked upon people's lives, especially my own and my family's; besides, anyone who boasts about their criminal activities, or about having hurt anyone in any sort of way, is a moron, plain and simple. Incidentally, I have not been high off anything in over seventeen years and I never will again. Not because I did not enjoy getting high. I loved smoking weed and shooting cocaine, but it occurred to me one day in a moment of clarity that my whole life revolved around getting high, and I no longer wanted anything controlling my life. I wanted to control it. It was this realization and the thought of not wanting to hurt anyone, my family, society or myself, ever again which drastically changed the direction of my life.

Fortunately, I still had enough sense left to also realize that I needed professional help, so I requested such, and for the next six years I received psychological counseling. My therapist told me at fthe conclusion of our first interview, that I had a major advantage over almost all his other patients, since I had requested therapy, whereas in the case of the others, the parole board had recommended that they seek it. The point here is, regardless of how many times you have been "down" or how much time you have served, nothing designed by man can make you change, because after everything is said and done to you, the choice is still yours and yours alone.

Keep the word "choice" in the forefront of your mind, because I will be referring to it throughout my presentation.

My therapist told me, at the start of my therapy, that I needed to know what were the three main character traits of the criminal mentality. First and foremost, is a lack of empathy. Simply defined, a lack of empathy means: we do not care how our actions will affect other people. If we want it, we will take it by any means necessary. Lie, cheat, steal, even put our mamas on an airplane with a time bomb in her luggage. Drown our children in a bathtub, or have a family member assassinated; all to collect the insurance money. Shoot a fifteen year old in the head, just to steal his Air Jordan's and fake gold neck chain. Commit an armed robbery, then murder the four high school girls working at a yogurt shop for less than three hundred dollars. Break into a blind and crippled senior citizen's house, to steal their social security check, then brutally rape and bludgeon them to death with a baseball bat.

If you are presently incarcerated, you are surrounded by people who have committed similar crimes of greater or lesser degree, but what is almost as bad as committing the crime itself is boasting about it to your peers. Then again, boasting about our criminal behavior is culturally acceptable in prison; after all, where else could we receive any sort of recognition for having used and abused someone except by another criminal.

The second main character trait of the criminal mentality is: rationalizing and/or justifying our criminal behavior. Here are a few of the general excuses we make:

"I was raised in a dysfunctional family."

"I was mentally, physically or sexually abused as a child."

"I was railroaded by the police, by the judge, by the prosecutor."

"The justice system is racist and unfair."

"My mother did not breastfeed me."

"I was poor and raised in the ghetto."

We also attempt to justify our criminal actions by down playing the types of crimes we commit. In other words, we make mindless statements such as:

"I only stuck up a liquor store, I am not a child molester."

"I only sold dope, my crime did not contain any violence."

"I was only charged with D.W,I., I did not car jack or home invade anyone."

One of the ways tat dope pushers try to down play their crime is by saying that they only provide what people want. That is an incredibly narrow-minded and stupid statement, because an addict will commit several crimes a day to support his habit. Let us be real and totally upfront with each other. Dope pushers are some of the worst parasites in our society, as they will sell their poison to anyone: children, teenagers, pregnant women, even the retarded. It is a slap in the face to all common sense to say that it is a crime without violence, because every time a crack head, meth head or heroin addict commits any sort of crime, the dope pusher, by proxy, is an accessory.

It goes without saying that child molestation is a horrendous crime; basically it is an attack on innocence, but again, it must be emphasized that the criminal mentality is always good at pointing the finger at everyone else except themselves. There is a psychological term that is called projection, which pinpoints this type of behavior, and it is quite common in prison. Generally, it is described in this manner: as long as I can keep the spotlight focused on you, it is not on me. For example: when a drug dealer sells crack to a pregnant woman, is he not abusing a child? When a dealer sells drugs to an underage addict who prostitutes herself to support her habit, did he not also abuse this child? This same drug dealer will point the finger at a person who molests children and call him a monster. In prison the pedophile is hated and despised, even beaten to death, while the drug dealer is glamorized and glorified. Am I the only one who recognizes that there is something terribly wrong with this picture?

It is an established fact that on a regular basis, drunk drivers are responsible for 70% of all traffic deaths, but because alcohol is interwoven into almost all aspects of our culture, people convicted of D.W.I. do not feel that their crime is of major consequence, even after multiple convictions. They say: "I'm not a thief, nor did I assault anyone."

What is amazing about their attitude, is that they refuse to recognize what could potentially happen every time they get behind the wheel of a car after having only a few drinks. If you also feel that driving under the influence of alcohol, or any other type of intoxicant, is not a serious criminal act, I assure you that if you ever have a friend or family member murdered by a drunk driver, or you knew someone who was horribly burned or paralyzed for the rest of their life, your sentiment about D.W.I. would drastically change.

The third main character trait of the criminal mentality is: being parasitic. Basically, it means to prey on or exploit the vulnerability of others.

To a greater or lesser degree, all criminals are parasites. Unfortunately, many of you are unaware that there is a sick and twisted segment of our culture that glamorizes crime and the so-called underworld; therefore, you have been brainwashed into believing that it is hip and in vogue to be a player, thug or thief.

The segment I am referring to is the multi-billion dollar entertainment industry. In particular, movies such as: Scarface, New Jack City, and Traffic have become pop icons.

One of the characters who is idolized by young men is Tony Montana. Tony was a Cuban refugee who came to America penniless. He thanked Uncle Sam for his hospitality by immediately getting involved in the drug world. Tony was brave, smart and ruthless. In a very short time he became a major player. Started wearing custom made suits, alligator shoes and driving a Porsche. But this was not enough, he wanted it all, what he called, "The Power". So he murdered his boss and became a drug lord. A multimillionaire. Had it all and then some.

The question, that the angels scream down from heaven is, "But what was he really?!" On the for real side, Tony was the head of a criminal enterprise which was responsible for bringing thousands of kilos of cocaine into this country.

For just a moment, stop and think about all the crimes, murders and other atrocities against humanity that will be committed behind the distribution of just one of these kilos. The lives it will devastate. The young men it will send to prison. The families it will destroy, and the women who will prostitute themselves to obtain it.

In every sense of the word, Tony Montana was a criminal monster, because he is an accessory to each and every one of these crimes.

If you want to know the depth of horror and wickedness that people will sink to in the drug world, think about this: a few years ago, a six month old baby was kidnapped in a shopping center in Rio de Janeiro. Five days later a couple and their alleged child were detained when they tried to cross the border, because one of the custom officers noticed that their child appeared to be sick. Upon further investigation it was discovered the child was actually dead and unusually heavy. Suspecting the absolute worst, they x-rayed it and discovered to their horror, that it had been gutted and stuffed full of cocaine. After a lengthy interrogation, the couple confessed to kidnapping the child in the shopping center, murdering it by strangulation, then removed its inner organs and filled it with five kilos of raw cocaine; furthermore, they had previously done this to four other children.

How would you have felt if this had been your child?

Still want to be a drug lord?

When someone represents himself as a player, actually boasts about it, what is he really proclaiming? He is saying he is out to use you in any capacity that he can get away with. A so-called player is even more of a parasite than a thief; however, by some twisted reason that contradicts basic common decency, young men idolize the character portrayed in the aforementioned movies and strive to become like them. Forgetting that underneath all the bling bling, coolness, glitter and flash, they are still nothing but wolves in sheep's clothing.

By the same token, when someone represents themselves as a thug, what is he really proclaiming? He is saying that he believes it makes him more of a man to act mean, hard and tough. To act, means to pretend, and a real man does not have to pretend anything.

So-called thugs have been tricked into believing that it is weak or passive to show any sort of basic manners, kindness, consideration or compassion toward anyone.

It is easy to spot a wannabe thug in any crowd, just look for the idiot holding his crotch, talking the loudest and acting like he could whip Godzillas. Every other word that comes out of his mouth is some sort of negative filth or sexual profanity towards women. He insinuates that they are nothing but a piece of pleasure meat. Calls them bitches and hoes, and believes that their sole purpose in life is to worship the ground he walks on.

What wannabe thugs seem to be obsessed with, as they talk about it more than anything else, is respect. Although they demand it and will quickly hurt you if they think that they have been even slightly disrespected, they actually give it less than anyone else.

One of the oldest axioms in the world is, "If you want respect you have to give it". The reasons that wannabe thugs are incapable of giving genuine respect, is because their whole persona is fake. It is fake, because their life style is so superficial, as it has no real honor, integrity or ethical code of conduct. It's a dog eat dog mentality.

Now that we are aware of how a criminal thinks and acts, the questions that we should be asking ourselves are: do I have such a mentality? And if so, what can I do to change it?

The change that I am talking about is not a pretentious or temporary one that is used to con the parole board into releasing you, or one that is fronted when you want to deceive someone. It is deep-rooted permanent change which will prevent you from ever having another negative contact with the authorities the rest of your life. Yes, it could really happen!

Earlier, I said that you should keep the word 'choice' in the forefront of your mind. If you are capable of understanding that this word has more influence over your life than any other, then you are ready to be the captain of your fate and the master of your destiny. Someone very wise once said, "In order to know where you are going, you have to know where you have been." By knowing "where you have been" we are able to recognize that every choice and every decision we have ever made in our entire life is linked together in a chain of events, and this chain has led us to the present moment. Where we go from here, the direction our life takes, will lie solely on the choices we make.

One of the most elite minds that has ever been on this planet, was a Jewish psychiatrist named Viktor Frankl. During the Second World War while he was an inmate in Auschwitz, which was one of the Nazi death camps that were scattered throughout Europe, he had a very profound realization about choices, which he called: "The last of the human freedoms". The realization occurred when he was sitting alone in a room that was filled with numerous skeletal like bodies which were destined for the crematory ovens. He thought, "Even in this situation I still have the freedom to choose my response to it." What made his thought so profound was that he had it while being systematically starved to death, and subjected to some of the worst atrocities that have ever been perpetrated against humanity.

Each of us can do what Dr. Frankl did. This is, we can choose our own response to whatever situation we are faced with; furthermore, we can also choose our response to whatever is said or done to us. After all, the one thing that can never be taken away from you is your freedom of choice.

One of the most sought after and highest paid speakers in the world is Stephen Covey. He wrote a book entitled: "The Seven Habits of Highly Effective People", which has sold over 27 million copies worldwide. In this book he took Dr. Frankl's "Last of the Human Freedom Principles" to an even higher level, saying, "The quality of your life is determined in the space and/or moment in between the stimulus and response".

For clarity's sake, we need to understand that the stimulus is anything that is said or done to you, anything you encounter, any situation. The response is the choice or decision you make to the stimulus. Therefore, whatever state your life is presently in (the quality of it) was directly caused by the choices and decisions you made.

Everything that I have mentioned so far is a good example of the stimulus-quality of life-response principle. That is to say, my presentation has been the stimulus, and each and every one of you will consciously choose a response to what I have said. Others, the players amongst you, will choose to think that they are so clever, slick and full of game, no one can tell them a damn thing about getting over. They know how to beat the system.

A few of you will somewhat take into consideration what I have said, maybe even make a half-hearted commitment to start making better choices; unfortunately, in a short while you will revert back to your old foolish life style of making one bad decision after another because you do not have the strength of character to keep your word, even to yourself.

A small percentage of you, the ones that have not been completely brainwashed yet, still have enough sense to recognize that I'm trying to spare you from the long years of suffering, humiliation and shame that I had to endure, because I thought that everyone was full of the smelly stuff, no one could tell me a damn thing, and I could keep my word even if my life depended on it.

When I was in my early twenties, another very wise person told me something which I now consider some of the most intelligent advice I ever received. He said: "If you cannot say no to whatever, then you deserve to whatever happens to you." Without question, this is a pretty hard core and matter-of-fact statement. Nonetheless, it is as real, as real can get. When I look behind me on the road I have traveled, and I truthfully apply what he said to my own life I can think of a million and one times I wish with all my heart that I would have said no. It was not because I was incapable of saying no. We have already shown that I had the freedom of choice to do this at every opportunity, but I chose not to. I now (nearly forty-two years later) clearly understand my reasons for not doing this.

First and foremost, it was because I cared more about what other people thought of me, than what I thought of myself. People who are insecure, have identity crisis, and possess weak and shallow characters, think in this sort of manner.

It s difficult for anyone to admit that they are insecure, or have a weak character, but there is an easy way to tell—a sort of measuring stick—to determine if you do or not.

There is a pretty good possibility that within a short time span, someone (more likely it will be a so-called friend) is going to proposition you to do something that your better judgment will advise you not to do, but you will not listen to your inner voice of reason. Instead, you will do whatever is suggested (regardless of the consequences) because you do not want them to think that you are some sort of geek, chump, or lame with no game.

Here is the measuring stick; on one hand, the more you listen to these sort of foolish propositions, the less secure you will be with yourself. On the other hand, the more you listen to your inner voice of reason, the more secure you will be, because every time you do not listen, it weakens your character. Here is a good way to remember what I just said: If you allow a fool to make you part of his problem, what does this make you? Answer: A fool's fool.

Here are two more measuring sticks that will greatly improve the quality of your life if you apply them. The first is: The hardest no you can ever say is to yourself, but every time that you do, you grow stronger. That is, because like a savings account, you are depositing no's into your memory bank, which you can then refer back to when you are tempted to ignore your inner voice of reason and do something stupid. In other words, since you were able to say no to whatever yesterday, you are capable of saying no to whatever today. Does this make sense?

The second is: true friendship should be measured by its intentions. That is to say, if any so-called friend suggests, propositions or tries to entice you into doing anything which could cause you any sort of harm, then they are not your friend. Real friends will always have your best interest at heart; furthermore, rational sense dictates that, if you hang with a lame you going to end up limping. There is an abundant proof of that statement, because prisons are full of people who did not give a damn about who they associated with.

Several years ago I had the privilege of meeting a Zen master, and he asked me a question, which profoundly affected my life. Actually, the question contained two parts. The first part was: "What did I want more than anything else?" And the second, "Why did I want it?"

The master went on to say that I should bear in mind that the second part of the question is just as important as the first part, because most people want things for other people's approval, or acceptance. In other words, I want a nice car, diamond watch or big house so that you can see me with it and be envious of what I have.

At that period of my life I didn't have the foggiest notion what I wanted more than anything else, but this question so intrigued me that it triggered a deep yearning (almost an obsession within me) to find out.

After a considerable amount of soul searching, I decided that I wanted a complete honor with myself and my life. I wanted it, or I should say I needed it, because I had no point of reference to live from. The question that then preoccupied my mind was, how did I go about acquiring complete honor with myself and my life?

I had once read about an honor system that they have at the West Point Military Academy. When you enter it, you take an oath to report any dishonesty. Failing to do this, means you have committed treason against their code of honor.

Having been an outlaw the majority of my life and practically raised in the penitentiary, it was difficult for me to come to terms with this concept, because it had been driven into my head that the one thing you didn't do, under any circumstances, was snitch. Even if you were snitched on, you did not retaliate in like manner.

What I failed to understand about their code, was that it was an absolute statement, a declaration, that they were not going to tolerate any substandard behavior (lying, cheating of failure of duty), and since you are part of the academy itself, neither will you accept any substandard behavior either.

There is a deeper meaning, a psychological one, as to why these cadets are taught to live by a code of honor. It is because it is the quality of character that all men respect and admire above all others.

Throughout history, in every country and culture, it has been proven in warfare that men will give their loyalty to a man of honor. He does not have to be braver, smarter or tougher than them, but if he is an honorable man, they will give their all in all and follow him to death.

For clarity of our topic we need to define what a honorable man is. Basically, it is someone who is fair minded, has strong morals, and makes a diligent effort to do what is right regardless of the consequences.

When I told the master that I had found what I wanted more than anything else, he said, "Know this and know it well, honor is something that must be earned, but if you pursue it with all your heart and all your soul it is a path which will lead you to heaven."

He then asked me another mind boggling question, which also took me a considerable while to answer. The question was: "What was the most important moment of your life?"

For several days I pondered that question, then it dawned on me that the moment I was conceived—when the sperm cell and egg combined and the miracle of new life was created—that had to be the most important, but he shook his finger at me signifying that it was not. He then pointed to the space in front of us and said, "This is the most important moment of your life, because it is the only one that exists. Yesterday is gone and tomorrow is not here."

At that moment my consciousness was more aware than it had ever been, because I realized that the war with myself could be conquered, if I took the responsibility to do what was right in the present moment, as it was the only one I had control over. I could not change the past, but the choices I made in the now, would affect what would happen in the next moment and the one after that. Therefore, I could, to some extent, control my destiny.

Again, throughout history in every culture and civilization, great thinkers and men of wisdom have advised us to listen to our father mind, our moral voice of reason, as it will always tell us the right thing to do. As a student of human nature, I'm curious why we so often ignore that voice. I did for the majority of my life, and severely suffered the consequences for not listening. If you want to know how much attention you are paying to your own voice, all you have to do is truthfully examine the present state of your life.

If you have been listening closely, you should by now have a clear and practical understanding of how your whole life revolves around the choices you make. It is self-evident that every time your inner voice of reason speaks to you, you will make a choice to listen or ignore it, and if you continue to ignore it, then you are going to keep getting what you have been getting and the quality of your life will never improve.

There is another very powerful word which will also give you much more control over your life, and that word is discretion. Basically, it means to know when to speak and when to shut up, when to move and when not to. It is also to your advantage to bear in mind, that if you are going to speak, be aware of what you should say or not say, and if you are going to act, consider the appropriate action. In almost every situation you can say too much, or not enough, or you can underact or overact, but whatsoever you do or say, there will be a reaction. It is the reaction and/or response that you need to start being more conscious of.

Many years ago while I was talking to my mother on the phone, I said to her: "It seems that the more that I think about what I'm about to say, the less I say." Her response was, "That is about the smartest thing I have ever heard you say."

Children have practically no discretion. That is because they are still learning the proper way to speak and act. It is very easy to tell how mentally mature someone is, just listen to what they say and watch how they conduct themselves. If they have a me, me me mentality, or a do not give a damn attitude, or they are loud, ill-mannered and disrespectful, then they are still a child trapped inside an adult's body. Although they are not aware of it, children have a selfish nature and want to be the center of attention. It is all about: see me, look at me, notice me. On one hand, children are not yet mature enough to realize that all their actions will produce a reaction. On the other hand, only an adult can develop a do not give a damn attitude, because his personality has become retarded. Prisons are full of retarded personalities.

Just before I got out of prison on my last sentence, a parole board member came to one of our college classes as a guest speaker. When a fellow student asked her, "How do you evaluate an inmate's conduct while he was down?"

Here is what she said, "The way you are acting now is the same way that you will act in the free world, because your character and behavior is not going to change overnight. So if you can not follow simple rules and regulations in here, you are not going to do it out there. Actually, you will be worse out there, because you will not have someone telling what to do 24/7, you will be expected to be self-checked like every other adult citizen in our society."

Here is another measuring stick to judge your own behavior with. A man, a grown man, never has to be told what to do, or how to act. He knows and conducts himself appropriately. In other words, he is self-checked. I'm not talking about the fool who constantly claims to be a man, but still conducts his affairs like a child. I'm talking about someone who is responsible for himself, because nothing says more about you than your personal accountability.

Prisons are full of little boys demanding to be treated as men, but they are under an illusion as to how a man is supposed to carry himself. To a certain extent it is not completely their fault, because (again) our culture and entertainment industry has led them to believe that they have to act like they are some sort of macho, chauvinistic bully to be a man.

One of the most cowardly things a man can do, is to put hands on a woman. That is because in a one-on-one fight she cannot win. Nevertheless, we have been physically abusing and beating to death our women since the dawning of time.

Unless they are mentally and emotionally deranged, no one likes to be hurt, but it is common to hear men say, "I've got to go upside her head every now and then to keep her in line." Or, "She likes it when I beat that ass." You would have to be either brain-dead or a complete idiot to believe such nonsense.

Since men possess the strength and the larger size, they are supposed to be the protectors of women, not their antagonists. Restraining your own physical abuse is part of this protection.

Not only are men the front line defenders of the community, they are also the head of the household; therefore, they are obligated to set the moral example for the entire family to follow. Bearing in mind that the best teacher of all is not what you tell them, it is what they see you do which will make the greatest impression.

The board member who came to my class was asked another question, and her answer will prove most beneficial if you apply it to your life. The question was: "What is your best advice for not returning to prison?" She said: "On a regular basis, there is a small percentage of people who come to prison, experience its humiliation, get out and never return. The question here is, what is the one thing they all have in common that is keeping them out? I am convinced that it is because they changed their attitude. So my very best advice to you is: stop acting and thinking like the people around you. Whatever direction you see the inside crowd moving towards, go in the opposite direction. If you return to the free world with the same mentality that you came with, more than likely you will be back and you will keep coming back until you get your heart right or we break it. The choice is entirely yours."

I agree with almost everything she said, except on this one point: the mentality that you come to prison with, could now be more criminally inclined. Here is how you can tell. Everyone in prison fantasizes about what they want to do when they get out. If you envision yourself becoming some sort of drug lord—of the Tony Montana type—or an Iceberg Slim with a stable of hoes at your beck and call, or an international player, living of your wits and always staying just one step ahead of the cops, then you will probably spend the rest of your life in and out of prison. However, if you envision yourself having a legitimate career, living a crime-free life, raising a family, being active in your church and community, then you could be in that small percentage who manages to never come back. I said all the above to say this: you can make the choice to stop being stuck on asshole.

If you have not listened to anything I have said so far, listen to this, I mean really tune into what I'm about to say, because it will save you from a lot of misery.

Forty-two years when I started my criminal career of being stuck on asshole, remember I spent over thirty-three of them in the pen, no one took the time to talk to me in the straightforward manner in which I have talked to you. In other words, no one took me as deep into the game as I have taken you; therefore, you have got a major advantage over what I never had, because you have been given a detailed road map of where not to go, straight out of the horse's mouth. So from this day forward you can not claim not to know what will happen to you if you do not make the choice to permanently change your self-destructive life style, or as the board member said, your attitude. By now there should not be any doubt in your mind on where to start. It begins with you saying no to whatever has the potential of hurting you, your family or society. It begins with you listening to your own inner voice of reason, the next time it screams or whispers at you not to do whatever, and it begins when you fully realize that your "get money or die trying" attitude is nothing but a death wish. That your fantasy of wanting to become a pimp, player or gangster, makes you nothing more than a vampire, a parasite and a failure as a man and a human being.

Here is an experiment that I can certainly guarantee you the results: make a list of the ten hippiest people that you know, who are presently involved or who plan on being involved in the so-called underworld. These ten people are the ones you think really represent the game and are true players. Now put the list away safe for the next twenty years, then come back and review it. Let us hope you did not add yourself to the list, because I will bet you and give you ten-to-one odds that at least nine of the ten on your list are either dead or in the penitentiary.

One of the reasons for this is, there is a whole lot of reverse psychology being pumped into your head. That is to say, just because the words sound clever, Mack Daddy or Fly, does not mean the message is not nonsense. Here is a perfect example: "Don't be a player hater." What is really being implied here? The player, AKA the roach, or leech, is trying to camouflage his use of someone with this wannabe slick slogan. He is saying, do not hate me because I'm a parasite who is out to use anyone I can get away with. Do not hate me because I give less than a damn about doing what is right. I'm going to get what I want by whatever means is necessary, and if I step on you, your family or the laws of our society while I'm stacking my paper, then so be it, "Cause I've got to have mine!" Well, in the sight of God, it is not yours unless you have earned it righteously.

Here is something else that I guarantee you. Throughout the world, prisons are full of people who have this sort of "Got to have" attitude, and if you have a similar one, then you are going to get your proper due alright, but it is not going to be the one that you want, it will be the one that your hand calls for.

It has been said that you can lie to the whole world, but you cannot lie to yourself. That is a powerful truth, so is this: you can become such a good con artist, that you can also con yourself into believing almost anything.

I hope that I have not given anyone the impression that I think I have got it all together, or that I know all the answers, I make no such claims, but I do know this, if I do not know anything else: whatever road you are presently traveling, you are on it because you have chosen to be on it, and you can get off it anytime you choose. No one has a gun to your head making you walk it.

There are higher roads in this life to travel. Roads that are filled with light, so you never have to look over your shoulder. Roads that have no shadows, so you can walk them without shame. Roads that are paved with self-respect and honorable accomplishments. Roads that lead to heaven.

Do you love your life enough to change it?
Peace Be With You.

About the Author

Truus Geraets has dedicated her life to work with people, the healthy or the sick, the young or the old, the free or those incarcerated. The inspiration for her work comes from the volume of work by Rudolf Steiner and its practical applications in Waldorf Education, Education for the "Handicapped" and the Healing Arts (Eurythmy). She is the author of two books:" Courage and Love for Children in South Africa" and "Inkanyezi". Two other books are "The Healing Power of Eurythmy" and its German translation.

More can be found on her websites: www. healingartofliving.com and www.waldorfforafrica.org

Notes

Chapter One
Page

1   Eurythmy—Art of Movement—inaugurated by Rudolf Steiner in 1912 and practiced as an art on stage, in education and as a healing agent.

2   Anthroposophy, a body of knowledge, encompassing all fields of human endeavor, seen from a spiritual scientific perspective by Rudolf Steiner

3   "Eurythmy, Essays and Anecdotes", Schaumburg Publications, Roselle, IL 1981

7   Viktor Frankl, "Man's Search for Meaning", Beacon Press, Boston, 1962
Viktor Frankl, "The Will to Meaning", New American Library, New York, 1969

10   "Logotherapy", a type of existentialist analysis, developed by Viktor Frankl, which focuses on the Will to Meaning
Rudolf Steiner, "Philosophy of Spiritual Activity", a Path to Self-Knowledge, 1984

12   33 Ways to Play a Loser's Game, see Appendix

Chapter Six

Chapter Seven

Chapter Eight

Chapter Nine

Chapter Ten